Ethnic minorities in urban areas

A case study of racially changing communities

David P. Varady
University of Cincinnati

Martinus Nijhoff Publishing
Boston / The Hague / London

Sole distributors for North America:
Kluwer Boston Inc.,
160 Old Derby Street,
Hingham, MA, 02043, USA

Library of Congress Cataloging in Publication Data
Varady, David P
  Ethnic minorities in urban areas.

  Bibliography: P.
  Includes index.
    1. Residential mobility--Pennsylvania--Philadelphia
--Case studies. 2. Philadelphia--Race relations--Case
studies. I. Title.
HD7304.P5V37   301.45'1'0420974811   78-10876
ISBN 0-89838-013-8

ISBN 90 207 0803 1

Distributors outside of North America:
Kluwer Academic Publishers Group
Distribution Centre
P.O. Box 322
3300 AH Dordrecht, The Netherlands

Acknowledgements

This volume dates back to spring, 1969 when I was a doctoral student in city planning at the University of Pennsylvania and also a staff member of the Center for Research on the Acts of Man. The leaders of Beth Zion Temple, a large Conservative congregation in Wynnefield (a racially changing community) in Philadelphia,[1] approached Dr. Samuel Z. Klausner to consider conducting research related to two questions: (1) Should the congregation remain at its current location and (2) If not, where should it relocate to? I was appointed to direct the study. During the spring and summer of that year, a random sample of Jewish and non-Jewish families were telephone interviewed for religious, demographic and mobility information. Later that year, Jewish families who were telephone interviewed were sent and completed mailed questionnaires dealing with Jewish cultural and religious characteristics. The results of these surveys were reported on in a technical report to the congregation titled *Synagogues Without Ghettos*. My section of the report dealt with mobility and migration patterns of the different religious groups in the area and the extent to which these patterns were likely to alter the population composition of the area.

The experience of writing this section excited my interest in the subject of neighborhood racial change. As a result, I chose as my dissertation topic, *The Household Migration Decision in Racially Changing Neighborhoods*. Utilizing the same data set that was used in the report to Beth Zion Temple, I focused on four issues: (1) the characteristics of the racial transition process; (2) whether white households accelerated moving plans in response to racial change; (3) factors affecting moving plans; and (4) factors affecting attitudes toward residential integration.

In the fall, 1973, the Institute for Jewish Policy Planning and Research (Washington, D.C.) provided a grant to the Center for Research on the Acts of Man which made it possible to re-survey the Jewish families who had been interviewed in 1969. This volume is based on the results of both the 1969 and 1974 surveys.

---

1. The identity of the congregation has been masked to protect its anonymity.

Many people assisted me in preparing this monograph. I am indebted to Samuel Z. Klausner for teaching me the methods of survey research and for the opportunity to direct the original 1969 study. He has also provided a detailed critique of each of the chapters in this volume. Other members of the staff at the Center for Research on the Acts of Man provided invaluable assistance in completing the 1969 and 1974 surveys.

This volume also benefits from the comments I received from members of my dissertation committee: Dr. Howard Mitchell, Dr. Martin Rosenzweig and Dr. Morton Schussheim. I am especially grateful to Dr. Paul Niebanck, supervisor of the dissertation, who guided me in conceptualizing the problem and provided encouragement throughout.

My colleagues at the Graduate Department of Community Planning at the University of Cincinnati have made this an ideal working environment for writing this monograph. I want to especially thank Dr. Kenneth Corey, Chairman of this department for his critiques of several of the chapters as well as for his willingness to be a sounding board for my ideas. I also appreciate the statistical advice I have received from Dr. William Philliber (formerly of the Department of Sociology, University of Cincinnati), Dr. Al Tuchfarber (Department of Political Science, University of Cincinnati) and Dr. George Galster (Department of Economics, Wooster College). My student assistants have done much of the computer work and the preparing of maps: Pierce Eichelberger (Geography), Bruce Laybourne (Sociology), Ellyn Cohen (Graduate Department of Community Planning), and Connie Hinitz-Washofsky (Graduate Department of Community Planning). The Southwestern Ohio Regional Computer Center (SWORCC) facilitated this research by making sufficient computer time available to me. Finally, I want to thank Mrs. Debbie Keene and Mrs. Angela Dunphy for their careful typing of numerous drafts of this volume.

I would also like to thank Mr. Ira Silverman and Mr. George Johnson (former Director and former Research Director) of the Institute for Jewish Policy Planning and Research for their suggestions and encouragement. Without the financial support provided by the Institute, this volume would not have been possible.

I am especially grateful to the men and women in the Wynnefield-Lower Merion Township area who completed the telephone interviews and mailed questionnaires. Hopefully, the results of this monograph can be used by synagogues, churches and other ethnic institutions to improve the quality of life in this and similar areas.

My wife Adrienne helped me in textual editing and in preparing some of the maps. For this help and the moral support provided, I am deeply appreciative.

A somewhat different version of Chapter 4 has appeared under the title, 'White Moving Plans in a Racially Changing Middle-Class Community,' in the *Journal of the American Institute of Planners*, Vol. 40, No. 5, September, 1974. Chapters 5 and 6 appear in similar form in volumes 7 and 8 of *Regional Science Perspectives* under the titles, 'The Ethnic Factor and Moving Decisions in a Racially Changing Community,' and the 'The Mobility Process in a Racially Changing Community.'

Table of contents

Acknowledgements V
List of tables XI
List of figures XV
1. Introduction 1
2. Previous research: The underlying causes of neighborhood
   change 14
3. The racial transition process: Is Wynnefield a typical changing
   community? 38
4. Determinants of moving plans: Did white residents panic move? 67
5. Determinants of mobility: Do ethnic variables influence the decision to move? 84
6. The mobility process: Why householders think they moved ... 102
7. Synagogues and churches in changing communities: What role can
   they play in stabilization efforts? 120
8. Conclusions and policy implications 134
APPENDIX 1. Sampling scheme 143
APPENDIX 2. Biases introduced by sampling and interviewing proce-
            dures 147
APPENDIX 3. Additional statistical analyses for chapter four, deter-
            minants of moving plans 151
APPENDIX 4. Additional statistical analyses for chapter six, deter-
            minants of mobility 161
APPENDIX 5. Additional statistical analyses for chapter seven, at-
            titudes toward synagogue involvement in neighbor-
            hood stabilization efforts 167
References 173
Index 181

List of tables

CHAPTER THREE

Table 1.	Racial changes in Wynnefield – 1960 to 1970	43
Table 2.	Income and expenses of the Wynnefield Residents Association – 1967 to 1974	46
Table 3.	Comparison of Wynnefield whites and blacks with respect to selected socio-economic and housing characteristics – 1970 (tracts 117, 118 and 119 only).	49
Table 4.	Comparison of white and black Wynnefield families with respect to stage in life cycle	51
Table 5.	Changes in the socio-economic characteristics of Wynnefield's population between 1960 and 1970	51
Table 6.	Comparison of white and black Wynnefield families with respect to family structure controlling for family type (proportions of families that are single-headed)	54
Table 7.	Comparison of white and black Wynnefield families with respect to income controlling for family type (proportions of families with incomes of $ 10,000 or higher)	54
Table 8.	Comparison of white and black Wynnefield families with respect to tenant status controlling for family type (proportions of families who are homeowners)	55
Table 9.	Capacity and enrollment in Wynnefield schools 1974	59
Table 10.	CAT test scores for Wynnefield schools 1974	59
Table 11.	Incidence of crime in Wynnefield, the 19th police district (which includes Wynnefield)	62
Table 12.	Incidence of crime in Lower Merion Township – 1960, 1965, 1973	62

CHAPTER FOUR

Table 1.	Results of regression analyses relating moving plans (likelihood of remaining) with different personal characteristics and location for white respondents in the study area as a whole	74
Table 2.	Results of regression analyses relating moving plans (likelihood of remaining) with different personal characteristics for white respondents in Wynnefield and Lower Merion Township	76
Table 3.	Results of regression analyses relating moving plans (likelihood of remaining) with personal characteristics (including Jewish cultural characteristics) for Jewish Wynnefield respondents	82

CHAPTER FIVE

Table 1.   Simple associations and relative importance of background
characteristics in predicting moving plans (likelihood of remaining 3 years or more) and mobility (likelihood of remaining
between 1969 and 1974) for Jews in Wynnefield 94

CHAPTER SIX

Table 1.   Home and neighborhood related reasons for moving from the
1969 location 106
Table 2.   Family related reasons for moving from the 1969 location .. 109
Table 3.   Housing and neighborhood related reasons for choosing the
new location 110
Table 4.   Communities considered in selection of new location 113
Table 5.   Location of new home, by community area, by 1969 location 116

CHAPTER SEVEN

Table 1.   Proportions of Beth Zion members approving different policies
aimed at attracting members 124
Table 2.   Results of regression analyses relating attitudes toward community involvement with different personal characteristics for
Jewish respondents in Wynnefield and Lower Merion Township 126
Table 3.   Proportions of Wynnefield and Lower Merion Township Jews
approving different forms of synagogue community involvement 128
Table 4.   Relationship between changes in attitudes toward biracial
community action and location (1969) 130
Table 5.   Results of regression analyses relating changes in attitudes toward biracial community action with different personal characteristics 131

APPENDIX ONE

Table 1A. Proportions of Wynnefield and Lower Merion Township telephone samples interviewed 144

Table 1B. Proportions of synagogue sample and total Jewish sample completing and not completing mailed questionnaire 145

Table 1C. Response status of families sent Wave 2 mailed questionnaire 146

APPENDIX TWO

Table 2A. Comparison of families returning and not returning Wave 1
questionnaire 149

Table 2B. Comparison of families returning and not returning Wave 2
questionnaire 150

APPENDIX THREE

Table 3A. Results of crosstabular analyses relating moving plans (likelihood of moving) with location and personal characteristics for
white respondents in the study area as a whole 152

Table 3B. Results of crosstabular analyses relating moving plans (likelihood of moving) with selected personal characteristics for white
respondents in Wynnefield and Lower Merion Township 154

Table 3C. Inter-correlations of independent and dependent variables for
total sample of white respondents, Wynnefield and Lower Merion Township 156

Table 3D. Inter-correlations of independent and dependent variables for
white Wynnefield respondents 157

Table 3E. Inter-correlations of independent and dependent variables for
white Lower Merion Township respondents. 158

Table 3F. Results of crosstabular analyses relating moving plans (likelihood of moving) with Jewish cultural characteristics for Jewish
Wynnefield residents 159

Table 3G. Inter-correlations of independent and dependent variables for
Jewish Wynnefield respondents 160

APPENDIX FOUR

Table 4A.   Tests for reproducibility and scalability of sets of items includ-
                ed in the regression analyses   162
Table 4B.   Results of crosstabular analyses relating moving plans (likeli-
                hood of moving) and mobility (likelihood of moving) with per-
                sonal characteristics for Jewish residents of Wynnefield   163
Table 4C.   Inter-correlations of variables in regression analysis   166

APPENDIX FIVE

Table 5A.   Relationships between background characteristics and atti-
                tudes toward community involvement and neighborhood stabi-
                lization   168
Table 5B.   Inter-correlations of independent and dependent variables in
                regression analyses of determinants of attitudes toward syna-
                gogue involvement in biracial community activities and efforts
                to attract Jewish families to the Wynnefield area   169
Table 5C.   Relationships between background characteristics and the like-
                lihood of becoming more/less interested in biracial community
                action between 1969 and 1974   170
Table 5D.   Inter-correlations of independent and dependent variables in
                regression analyses of determinants of changes in support for
                synagogue involvement in biracial community activities   172

List of figures

CHAPTER ONE

Figure 1. Boundaries of study area 10
Figure 2. Population density Wynnefield 1960 11
Figure 3. Housing type 12

CHAPTER TWO

Figure 1. Elements affecting the decision to seek a new residence 33

CHAPTER THREE

Figure 1. Distribution of non-white population 1950 41
Figure 2. Distribution of non-white population 1960 42
Figure 3. Blacks 44
Figure 4. Distribution of religious groups 47
Figure 5. Black and white population by age 50
Figure 6. Changes in the racial composition of schools serving Wynne-
           field 57
Figure 7. Vacant dwelling units 60

CHAPTER FIVE

Figure 1. Mobility model 85
Figure 2. Path analysis of the effects of different background characteris-
           tics and moving plans on residential mobility (likelihood of
           remaining) among Wynnefield Jewish residents 96

CHAPTER SIX

Figure 1. Inter-census tract mobility 117

1. Introduction

1.1. The problem

Changes in the composition of American neighborhoods have occurred frequently during this century. Human ecologists, borrowing concepts from plant and animal ecology, have described these changes, utilizing the concepts of invasion and succession. These two concepts have been used to describe such diverse phenomena as the conversion of residential areas to business and industrial zones, and changes in the ethnic composition of particular areas.

Earlier in this century, particular neighborhoods were successively occupied by members of different white nationality groups. Since the cutoff in foreign immigration in the 1920's, national origin has become less important as a differentiator of America's urban population, and spatially defined enclaves of ethnic groups have tended to disappear. (See for example, Duncan and Duncan, 1957; Taeuber and Taeuber, 1965.) In recent years, ecologists have studied invasion-succession sequences involving blacks and whites. Most typically, the direction of change is from largely white to largely black, but in a small number of communities – Brooklyn Heights and Park Slope (New York City), Georgetown and Adams-Morgan (Washington, D.C.) and Society Hill and Queens Village (Philadelphia), the direction of change has been from largely black to largely white (Rheinhold, 1977b).

The transition of many neighborhoods from largely white to largely black has contributed to a number of social problems.[1] The withdrawal of whites from areas subject to black inmigration, as well as the exclusion of blacks from all white areas, have resulted in the sharp patterns of residential

---

1. Not all segments of the population view racial changes (from white to black) as a problem. These changes enable middle income blacks to improve their housing conditions while remaining highly accessible to the social and cultural institutions serving the black community. Additional evidence that some blacks may view these changes positively is provided by a recent city-wide survey in New York City (Dionne, 1977). The results indicated that while blacks shared many of the misgivings of whites about life in the city, they viewed life in the city in a more favorable light then they did four years earlier. It is possible that blacks were more hopeful because of racial changes. White flight may have made it possible for blacks to participate in every aspect of the city's life.

segregation in the United States (Taeuber and Taeuber, 1965: 28-64). Residential segregation limits the possibilities for contacts between whites and blacks, and as a result, decreases the potential for social unity. Residential segregation has been seen to lead to a sense of confinement among ghetto residents which exacerbates all the other problems that affect these neighborhoods. As a result, the spatial separation of the races has been viewed as a serious threat to the stability of the society (U.S. National Advisory Commission on Civil Disorders, 1968: vii). Spatial separation also leads to other specific problems such as *de facto* school segregation, while segregated schools have been declared inherently unequal.

Furthermore, the movement of blacks to the suburbs that has occurred in recent years[2] has not led to decreased patterns of isolation. Instead, this shift has reflected an expansion of existing ghetto areas across city boundaries. For example, Cleveland's black ghetto has expanded into and through East Cleveland which is a distinct municipality; (see Arthur D. Little, 1969) and Washington, D.C.'s ghetto has expanded northeast into suburban Prince Georges County (Zehner and Chapin, 1974).[3] Glantz and Delaney (1973) in a study of 14 of the 18 largest metropolitan areas, found that the degree of segregation of blacks within particular suburban municipalities had not changed much between 1969 and 1970. Blacks were concentrated in the same suburban communities in 1970 as in 1960. Rabinovitz and Siembieda (1977) make a similar point based on a case study of Los Angeles. They note that while the proportion of blacks living in Los Angeles' suburbs increased markedly during this period (from 2.9 percent to 8.4 percent of the total) blacks did not 'open up the suburbs'. The shift to the suburbs occurred in two ways: (1) an extension of the Watts ghetto; and (2) an extension of Pasadena's ghetto in suburban Los Angeles into newer expanding areas. As a result in 1970, blacks were just as likely to live in predominantly black census tracts in the suburbs as in the city of Los Angeles.

In addition, racially changing suburban communities have experienced many of the same problems as their counterparts in the central city. For

2. 'Since 1970, blacks have increased their share of the suburban population from 4.5 to 5.1 percent and 4 million now live outside the central city' (*Ford Foundation Letter*: October 1, 1976).

3. This is not to say that *all* blacks who have moved to the suburbs have moved to neighborhoods contiguous to black areas. For a journalistic account of the experiences of some middle class black families who have moved into predominantly white suburban communities, see Delaney (1976a).

example, almost all of the suburban communities studied by Rabinovitz and Siembieda, despite differences in government stance and socio-economic mixture, experienced conflict over the integration of the public schools. Mt. Vernon (a suburb of New York City) has experienced this same type of conflict in its public schools (Moran: 1969). At the height of racial tensions, two students were arrested for throwing a Molotov cocktail into the high school cafeteria.

Racial succession patterns have also had serious impacts on specific white population groups. Frequently, blacks have entered white ethnic neighborhoods largely occupied by middle aged and elderly families with strong emotional attachments to their homes and neighborhoods. The mental anguish felt by such residents, when they are forced to relocate as the result of urban renewal, has been documented by Fried (1963). As noted by the Griers (1966: 93), 'no doubt much the same kind of agony is caused when long-established white residents feel "forced" to give up their homes in changing neighborhoods.'

The withdrawal of whites from racially mixed areas has had a particularly strong impact on the churches and synagogues located in these areas. These churches draw their members from the immediate surrounding area. When members start to move away, the churches are often forced to close, consolidate or relocate to another location. The impact of these changes on Jewish communities has been described in the following way: 'Jews in the inner city see themselves waging a desperate struggle for the survival of their communities and the viability of their religious and social institutions' (*Jewish Exponent*, October 30, 1970).

The following two examples dealing with the Mt. Airy section of Philadelphia (Gross, 1973) and the East Flatbush section of Brooklyn, New York (Chambers, 1976), illustrate the sharp impact that racial changes have had on synagogues in these areas.

The Jewish community in the Mt. Airy section of Philadelphia is in a state of flux. As of now, the area contains seven synagogues... Within a year, it will contain only four synagogues and there is a possibility that this number may be reduced by half. It appears that Jews are leaving the area in ever increasing numbers and that their communal institutions are following them.

... a decade ago, Temple Bnai Abraham (East Flatbush) attracted 700 Jews to Yom Kippur, yesterday it drew 30 devout men and women, all elderly. Their children and their friends, fearful of a changing neighborhood, have fled to other Jewish neighborhoods ... in Long Island and New Jersey.

The closing of synagogues obviously hurts those who use them regularly – particularly the poor and the elderly who are unable to move elsewhere. As the Mattapan study indicates, however (Ginsberg, 1975: 105), these closings also hurt non-religious families living in the area.

Although the majority of people admitted using the synagogues only on rare occasions such as the high holiday, the fact that they were there was important for them. 'Jews want to be close to a *shul* even if they don't use it!' Nothing symbolized more strongly the fact that the Jewish neighborhood has disappeared than the fact that the synagogue had closed down.

Racial changes (as well as the prospect of undergoing change) has become a source of tension between blacks and other white ethnic groups besides Jews. It is commonly believed that the resistance to black inmigration in white ethnic neighborhoods, is attributable to white racism. Friedman (1971) notes that the explanation is far more complex. Black move-ins pose a threat to property values, friendship patterns, homogenous ethnic churches, familiar landscape and shopping areas, 'all those things that ethnic Americans value.'

The Marquette community in Chicago illustrates the complex nature of this issue (Kneeland, 1977). This is a neighborhood of well-kept brick bungalows containing a melting pot of Irish, Poles, Germans, Italians and the nation's largest concentration of Lithuanians. The community became a symbol of racial confrontation in 1968 when the late Rev. Martin Luther King was hit in the head with a stone when he led a civil rights march through the community. Tensions have been fanned by the presence of followers of the late George Lincoln Rockwell, the American Nazi party leader. Most residents claim that they are not racist but fear the pattern of decline and abandonment that has occurred in the adjoining predominantly black Englewood Park district. This fear is particularly prevalent among members of the closely knit Lithuanian community which has its own hospital, churches, schools, cultural center, newspaper, sports and social clubs, etc. Stanley Balzekas, leader of the community stated:

Under the czars and the Communists, Lithuanians couldn't own land ... so this becomes a very important factor, land ownership becomes security. For those who fought the Nazis and then the Communists and then were in the displaced persons camps from 1945 to 1950 or 1951, this was like coming to a little Lithuania. This was like Utopia and it looks suddenly like it may be taken away from them.

A further reason for interest in the racial succession process is that it is often accompanied by declines in the quality of the housing. The South Bronx and Bushwick sections of New York City are cases in point. The South Bronx contained solidly Jewish neighborhoods during the 1940's and 1950's (Ferretti, 1977); Bushwick was a solid, well-kept German neighborhood up to 12 years ago (Kifner, 1977). When members of these ethnic groups moved away, they were replaced by lower income non-white families. This set off a cycle of abandonment and destruction which is still continuing. On one street in the South Bronx, only 9 of the original 51 buildings that existed in the 1940's remain, and most of these are abandoned. Furthermore, this pattern of ethnic change and housing deterioration is shifting to attractive middle class communities such as Bronx Park South where the housing constitutes an important economic resource for the city. Fried (1976a) emphasizes the quality of the housing in this community:

They were built in the 1920's and were good buildings, large buildings, impressive buildings. If they were standing in Paris or London or Moscow, they would be considered luxury apartments.

Thus, racial change, through its impact on housing abandonment has contributed to the fiscal crisis in New York City and similar cities by shrinking its tax base.

Community leaders in areas like Bronx Park South, interested in implementing housing conservation programs aimed at maintaining and upgrading the quality of the housing, are finding it difficult to do so because of population mobility associated with ethnic succession (Thompson, 1965: 317-318). A prerequisite for a successful conservation program is a population that will remain long enough at one location to recapture the investment that it has made in property improvements. If white households think that black invasion is inevitable, they may reduce property maintenance and home improvements to a minimum based on the assumption that renovation costs will not be easily recovered.

A number of governmental and nongovernmental bodies have sought to develop policies to prevent or inhibit racial transition. In some communities, local resident associations have sought to preserve mixed occupancy by maintaining or improving the physical standard of the neighborhood, and by appealing to residents not to panic move. A consultant to the City of Milwaukee proposed using legal devices (e.g., anti-blockbusting laws and ordinances) to prevent the white-to-black sequence (Greenleigh Associates, 1967: 26). In East Cleveland, a consultant proposed using governmentally assisted housing programs to achieve a stable racially mixed city (Arthur D. Little, 1969: 90). Willingboro, New Jersey forbid the posting of 'For sale' signs in the hope of stemming white flight (Oelsner, 1977). Along similar lines, New York State issued an order banning real estate brokers and sales people from virtually all methods of soliciting homes for sale throughout Brooklyn and Queens, New York City (Fried, 1976b). University City, Missouri (a suburb of St. Louis) has attempted to achieve stable integration by expanding the size of its police force and by improving the quality of its public services (Tobin, undated).

Few of these efforts have been successful and this has hindered planners in the development of new stabilization programs (Arthur D. Little, 1969: 90). In such a situation, social science research can be particularly useful in program development. On the basis of an analysis of the factors affecting racial transition, policymakers can better predict what types of programs will succeed or fail in attempts to inhibit or prevent transition.

Programs are ' ... developed with a view to the future state of affairs ... and are organized on the basis of a variety of assumptions about events yet to occur' (Kahn, 1969: 81). In order to develop policies dealing with racial transition, it is necessary to consider whether existing patterns of segregation are likely to continue into the future. More specifically, will there be an increased willingness amongst whites to remain in racially mixed areas. A forecast for the large increase in the number of stable racially mixed neighborhoods in the United States might be based on the presumed impact of increases in the level of educational attainment in the white population.[4] It might be assumed that an increase in the level of racial tolerance will be associated with increases in educational attainment, and that the increase in racial tolerance will lead to an increased willingness among whites to move into and remain in racially mixed areas.[5] Research can be utilized in evaluating the assumptions underlying different forecasts of residential settlement patterns of blacks and whites. For example, research may be directed to whether the level of racial prejudice is an important factor affecting the willingness of households to remain in or move into racially mixed areas, and whether a college education reduces the level of racial prejudice.

Up to this point in this chapter, we have focused on ethnically changing communities in the United States. A recent volume edited by Peach (1975) emphasizes the fact that this is a worldwide phenomenon. There is a striking resemblance between this process in American cities and the process in foreign cities, e.g., the replacement of Protestants by Catholics in Belfast, Northern Ireland, the replacement of Jews by southern Europeans (Greeks, Italians, Maltese) in Melbourne, Australia.

---

4. For an example of this viewpoint, see Rapkin and Grigsby (1960: 121).
5. This assumption will be examined in Chapters 5 and 6.

Furthermore, European cities have begun to experience ghetto problems, although to a lesser degree than American cities. During the 1950's and 1960's, Great Britain experienced a large scale immigration of West Indians and the overwhelming majority settled in London and the other major industrial cities. In London, West Indians congregated in three areas of the inner city characterized by deteriorating housing. British planners have been concerned that these areas would develop into ghettos comparable to those in American cities.[6] A recent study by Lee (1977) suggests that these fears are to a certain degree justified. Firstly, the boundaries of the West Indian ghetto have shifted outward toward the suburbs in a manner closely similar to the ghetto expansion patterns of American cities. Secondly, there is a problem of alienation among West Indian youth which parallels a well documented problem among black youths in American cities. The rioting that has taken place among West Indian youths at the Notting Hill Carnival in London (the largest Caribbean carnival in Europe) the last two years, may be a harbinger of even more serious disorders in British cities in the future (Reed, 1977a, b).

The Dutch may also have a budding ghetto problem among non-white immigrants. Black Surinamese who have settled in the Netherlands have clustered in the Bijlmermeer, a vast complex of long 10-story apartment buildings on the southeastern outskirts of Amsterdam (*New York Times*, October 1, 1974). 'One section, the Gliphove, is 80 percent Surinamese and has a rundown look for which the tenants and owners say each other is responsible.' The Dutch tried to prevent other buildings from becoming predominantly Surinamese by refusing to give immigrants applications for vacant apartments. This led to charges of discrimination. After a peaceful march on the Amsterdam City Hall, the Surinamese were allowed to stay.

Thus, planners on both sides of the Atlantic are faced with the dilemma of what to do about expanding immigrant concentrations. Should residents be dispersed away from these areas or should the quality of life in these areas be enhanced (i.e., a ghetto enrichment strategy)? Furthermore, if the latter strategy is chosen, what, if anything, can be done to insure that neighborhoods along the edge of these ghetto areas will not undergo complete turnover when non-white residents move into them?

---

6. The West Indian ghetto is not fully comparable to the black ghetto in American cities. Although the West Indian population is concentrated, West Indians do not constitute a majority of the population in any one community.

1.2. Methodology

This volume is based on a two-stage survey of residents of the Wynnefield-Lower Merion Township area, two middle to upper-middle class communities located along the western edge of Philadelphia (Figure 1). During the spring and early summer of 1969, a random sample of 943 families were telephone interviewed for background demographic and mobility information.[7] Later that summer, 269 of the Jewish families were sent and completed mailed questionnaires which obtained more detailed attitudinal information (e.g., Jewish cultural characteristics, race related attitudes). In the summer of 1974, these families were sent follow-up questionnaires which repeated many of the attitudinal items from the 1969 questionnaire and also included a series of questions on residential mobility behavior between 1969 and 1974; 154 were returned.

Wynnefield is a roughly two and a half square mile area in West Philadelphia containing about 20,000 people. Like other 'communities' in Philadelphia, Wynnefield does not have any officially designated boundaries. Nevertheless, there has always been a fairly high degree of consensus among residents regarding the community's boundaries: the city boundary to the north (City Line Avenue), a large park (Fairmount Park) to the east, railroad tracks to the south, and another residential community (Overbrook Park) to the west. The study area also included all of Lower Merion Township, which has a population of about 60,000 in an area roughly ten times as big as Wynnefield.

Both Wynnefield and Lower Merion are primarily residential areas. Wynnefield is divided into two sections on the basis of housing type and density (Figures 2 and 3). The northern half of the community, 'Upper Wynnefield' has a relatively low residential density and is characterized by single-family homes on half acre lots. The remainder of the community, 'Lower Wynnefield', is typified primarily by single-family row houses with some bi- and tri-plexes. Generally speaking, Lower Wynnefield most closely resembles older neighborhoods in innercity Philadelphia, while Upper Wynnefield resembles nearby sections of Lower Merion Township. Lower Merion Township is a low density suburban area with the density somewhat higher in the southeastern than the northwestern section. The township contains some of the most attractive residential sections in the Philadelphia area. The desirability of these locations stems from the fine

7. Appendix 1 describes the sampling scheme used in the study.

homes, the beautiful open space and the extraordinary accessibility to downtown Philadelphia by commuter railroad (the travelling time is between 15 and 30 minutes, depending on the distance involved).

1.3. Research objectives

This is a case study of one racially changing Jewish community – the Wynnefield community of Philadelphia. It examines the characteristics and causes of the racial transition process in this community. As we will see later, Wynnefield is typical of middle class communities that have undergone racial transition during the 1960's and 1970's. As a result, the findings of this case study should be helpful in understanding the nature and causes of the process in other such communities throughout the United States. This study also has a policy orientation. Based on an analysis of the causes and characteristics of the process, we will look at the implications for efforts by religious institutions as well as governmental bodies to stabilize racially changing communities.

1.4. Chapter outline

Chapter 2 reviews previous research dealing with the racial transition process and the factors affecting mobility decisions in racially changing communities. In Chapter 3, we seek to determine the extent to which the racial transition process in Wynnefield has been typical of that in other middle-class communities generally, and other racially changing Jewish communities in particular. This chapter focuses on three aspects of the racial transition process: (1) factors that made the community susceptible to racial change; (2) the impact of stabilization policies, particularly the activities of the local residents association on the rate of racial change; and (3) the impact of the racial succession process on the socio-economic characteristics of the community and on community standards (e.g., the quality of the local public schools).

In Chapters 4 through 6, the focus shifts from the neighborhood to the individual household level. Chapter 4 tests whether white families in Wynnefield accelerated their moving plans in response to racial change. It then tests for the importance of different demographic and housing characteristics in holding whites to the area. Finally, it examines the importance

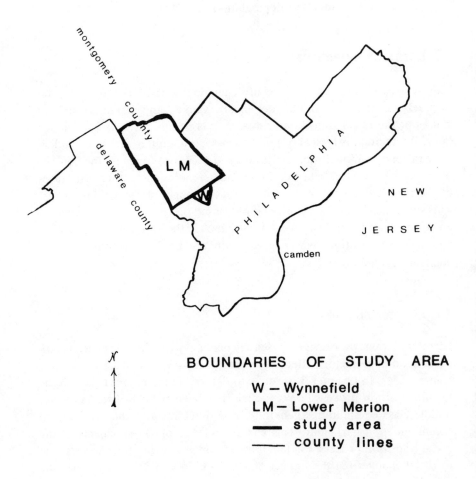

Figure 1. Boundaries of study area.

Source: Delaware Valley Regional Planning Commission.

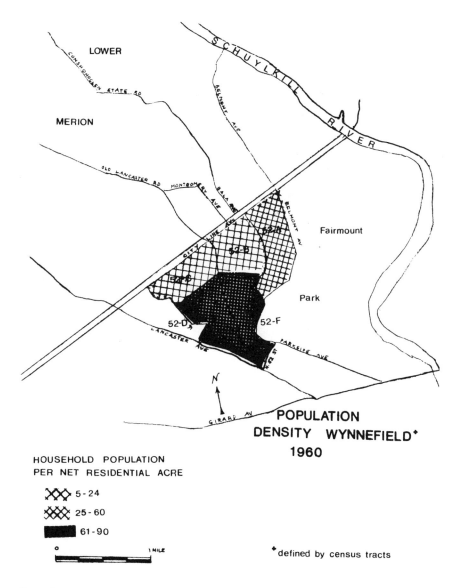

Figure 2. Population density Wynnefield 1960.

Source: U.S. Census 1960.

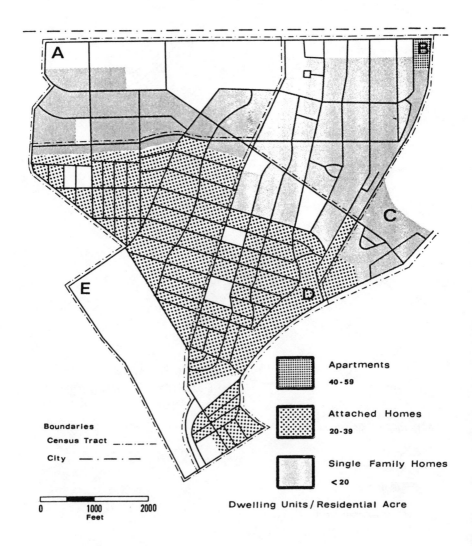

Figure 3. Housing type.

of two Jewish religious characteristics – Jewish denominational affiliation and frequency of synagogue attendance – in explaining variations in moving plans. Chapter 5 extends this analysis of the underlying causes of mobility by examining the relative importance of different race related attitudes, Jewish cultural characteristics and other background characteristics in explaining variations in mobility behavior among Jewish residents of Wynnefield. Chapter 6 looks at the motivations for moving from a different perspective; the perceived reasons for moving among those Jewish families who had moved.

While Chapters 3 through 6 examine the causes and characteristics of the racial transition process, Chapter 7 looks at a different subject, the degree of support among Jewish respondents for the involvement of the synagogue in community affairs (including stabilization efforts). Chapter 8 reviews the major findings of the study on the underlying causes of neighborhood racial transition and examines the implications of the findings for stabilization efforts in racially changing communities.

2. Previous research:
The underlying causes
of neighborhood racial change

2.1. Introduction

Beginning in the 1920's human ecologists utilized the concepts of invasion and succession borrowed from plant and animal ecology to explain changes in the ethnic composition of urban neighborhoods (Park, 1936a; 1936b; Hawley, 1950). These changes were assumed to follow basically the same laws whereby one plant or animal species replaces another in a given territory. According to the succession model, change results from the 'push' of increasing numbers of a new ethnic group which leads members of the more established group to move to a newer area closer to the periphery of the city (Burgess, 1928:112). Competition between the new and established group over land use is assumed to be an inherent aspect of the succession process – with competition often assuming the form of conflict (Park, 1936a).

Some ecologists such as Hoyt (1939) also emphasized that 'pull' factors play an important role in explaining ethnic change. As neighborhoods age they deteriorate physically and are perceived as obsolete by residents. At the same time attractive and fashionable neighborhoods are built closer to the edge of the city. The attraction of these newer areas (combined with social mobility and assimilation) 'pulls' the established ethnic group away from the older area.

During the 1920's and 1930's ecologists focused on neighborhood changes involving different white ethnic groups. A good example of this is Wirth's study (1928) of Chicago's first generation Jewish ghetto – the West Side.

In the course of the extension of the Jewish settlement, they encountered the Irish and the Germans. As these groups moved on, the Jews followed, only to be succeeded by the Italians, the Poles and the Lithuanians, the Greeks and Turks, and finally by the Negroes.

With the decline in foreign immigration and the increase in the number of blacks in cities, ecologists have focused their attention on shifts involving whites and blacks with relatively little attention given to the nationality of the whites (see for example, Duncan and Duncan, 1957; Taeuber and Taeuber, 1965).

This chapter reviews previous research dealing with the causes and characteristics of the neighborhood transition process. It seeks to identify those findings that are applicable to racially changing white middle-class communities. Two types of research are reviewed: ecological studies of the neighborhood transition process and studies of the decision to move of individual households in racially changing neighborhoods.

2.2. Ecological studies

2.2.1. Underlying causes of the transition process

Empirical research has established the importance of both pull and push factors in affecting neighborhood racial changes. 'Often it is held that whites leave a community before and during the change process for reasons having nothing to do with the issue of race; they are simply translating upward social mobility into geographical mobility' (Molotch, 1972:7; see also Ginsberg, 1975:153; Arthur D. Little, 1969:6). White outmigration has been facilitated by the availability of governmentally assisted mortgage financing and federal aid for highway construction. The withdrawal of established whites creates the opportunity for racial transition to occur. The process proceeds when pent-up black housing demand is focused on the area and all (or nearly all) of the homes made available by white withdrawal are taken by blacks.

Existing research does not support the assumption that racial transition necessarily involves conflict. Some communities have violently resisted black entry (Rose, 1969:16; Bressler, 1960; McFadden, 1976; Waldron, 1977 and Wooten, 1975), while others have quietly accepted black in-migration (Mayer, 1960; Northwood and Barth, 1965; Zehner and Chapin, 1974). Harold Rose (1970) notes that it is far more typical for whites to retreat from transitional areas than to compete over them.

The underlying cause of neighborhood racial transition is therefore the tendency for black ghetto areas to expand into and through previously predominantly white neighborhoods (Morrill, 1965; Rose, 1970). This pattern reflects the limited housing search behavior of blacks which is in turn a function of four factors: (1) white prejudice – the unwillingness of suburban whites to show their homes to blacks; (2) private institutional practices – the unwillingness of suburban realtors to show homes to blacks; (3) public institutional practices – the utilization of zoning and other means to limit the construction of low and moderate income housing; and (4) black attitudes – the desire among some blacks to maintain social ties and familiar patterns and contacts (Foley, 1973:92).

A neighborhood's proximity to black neighborhoods is the key factor affecting its vulnerability to black encroachment. White communities adjoining ghetto areas are most likely to experience high levels of black housing demand. Four other factors have been mentioned in the literature as playing a limited, but still significant role in affecting a community's susceptibility to black encroachment: (1) the cost and quality of the housing; (2) the age structure of the population; (3) the level of prejudice of the population; and (4) the community's ethnic composition (e.g., whether it is a Jewish community).

Ghetto expansion has usually occurred through communities consisting of moderately priced single family homes that are perceived by white residents as obsolete or unfashionable but which represent considerable improvement in housing quality for black arrivals (Wilkes, 1971; Arthur D. Little Inc., 1969; Molotch, 1972). On the other hand, apartment districts and areas of expensive housing (often located on hilly terrain) have been able to resist black encroachment despite proximity to expanding ghetto areas (Morrill, 1965). The latter finding reflects the fact that (1) the cost of the housing in these areas is usually beyond that of home seeking blacks; and (2) the fact that most of the home seeking black families have children and that this type of family usually has little interest in apartment living.

Transitional communities typically contain an aging white population (Wolf, 1965:33; Arthur D. Little Inc., 1969: 25-27; Wilkes, 1971; Ginsberg, 1975). Outmigration from these communities, prior to black inmigration tends to be selective of families in the child bearing and child rearing stages of the family life cycle and they are not replaced by similar families. Furthermore, it has not been unusual for the children of established residents in transitional communities to move to newer areas, rather than to remain in their 'old neighborhood.' The aging character of the population further contributes to the area's susceptibility to black encroachment. When the husband or wife dies, the spouse often puts the home up for sale in order to move to smaller quarters.

It has been frequently asserted by both laymen and social scientists that communities characterized by high levels of prejudice can successfully resist black encroachment (Freeman and Sunshine, 1970:76; Wilkes, 1971). Available evidence is far from conclusive. In a recent volume, Zehner and Chapin (1974) describe a white southern migrant community just outside Washington, D.C. which was experiencing a steady influx of blacks despite the fact that the population was characterized by a high level of prejudice. It might be argued that if prejudice is linked to violence this violence would cause blacks to move away and might dissuade prospective black residents from moving into the community (Molotch, 1972:7-8). Bradburn, et al., (1971:74) disagree, noting that those communities which have most strongly resisted black inmigration have been most likely to change from all white to all black. The effort to discourage blacks from moving in – to 'keep them out' – seldom succeeds, but it apparently leaves a legacy of anti-black bitterness or fear that encourages a rapid exodus of whites from the neighborhood.

The research literature provides conflicting evidence as to whether ethnic characteristics affect the likelihood that a community will undergo racial change. On the one hand, Simmons (1968: 633) in a widely quoted article notes, 'the ethnic factor acts as a constraint only on the number of possible alternatives, explaining "where" people move rather than "why" they move.' Although Simmons' article is at the individual family level, it would imply that there would be no differences in the susceptibility to racial change among various types of white ethnic communities. In fact, re-searchers have detected such differences.

Since the 1920's, social scientists have observed the tendency of the black ghetto to expand through Jewish neighborhoods rather than through other white ethnic communities (Burgess in Kain, 1970: 35; Rose, 1969: 16; Ginsberg, 1975: 150-54; Sobel and Sobel, 1966; Hodgart, 1968 mentioned in Lee, 1977: 81). There have been a variety of explanations of this pattern.[1]

---

1. In contrast to these other studies, Tobin (undated: 11) explains the stability of University City, (St. Louis) Missouri in terms of the presence of a large Jewish population. 'The liberal character of this ethnic group, a commitment at least in principle to integration by many Jews and a reluctance to abandon the traditional ethnic turf, prevented a short term panic of the largest sector of the University City population.' There are three weaknesses in Tobin's explanation, however, that limit its credibility. Firstly, he does not measure the relative importance of the ethnic composition of the population in comparison to other known strengths of the community in contributing to its stability (e.g., the excellent quality of the housing, the community's proximity to such large institutions as Washington University and the fact that the community is an independent municipality, separate from St. Louis, and therefore, able to be flexible in implementing stabilization policies. Had he measured the

Sklare (1972) suggests that the rapid withdrawal of Jews from older districts, often in the face of black inmigration, is attributable to (1) social mobility; (2) assimilation (i.e., the adoption of societal values emphasizing the suburban way of life); (3) Jewish family structure (i.e., the tendency for Jewish children to avoid living in the same neighborhoods as their parents); and (4) the lack of commitment of Jews to their physical environment.

...The Jewish neighborhood per se seems to have little symbolic or even actual significance for its residents, and its special facilities – synagogues, schools, kosher butchers, delicatessens, etc. – are looked upon as mere conveniences ... The explanation which first suggests itself for this attitude is that Jewish psychology has been conditioned by thousands of years of living in Exile, to react to situations of stress by a kind of avoidance behavior. Thus Jews did not feel that Brownsville, say, really belonged to them; when others claimed it, the Jews moved elsewhere.

Jews interviewed as part of Ginsberg's study of the Mattapan section of Boston (1975: 155) explained the vulnerability of Jewish communities as attributable to the fact that Jews do not fight back while members of other groups do. The respondents gave several additional reasons for the residential stability of their gentile neighbors and by implication, gentile neighborhoods (pp. 154-155). 'They want to live near the church; their leadership is stronger than that of the Jews; or education is not quite so important to them and anyway they send their children to parochial schools...Jews, on the other hand, "were all their life wandering, they didn't stay in one place!"'

Case studies of racially changing Jewish communities have indicated that within these communities, the Orthodox subcommunities tend to be the most stable. Johnson (1974:13) notes that an Orthodox congregation – consisting mostly of young professionals – in the racially changing Shepherd Park section of Washington, D.C. held on long after most of the Jewish population moved from the area. He attributes this to the strong bonds within the group as well as their desire to meet religious needs (e.g., to be within walking distance of a synagogue). Wolf (1965) asserts that one reason for the relatively low rate of racial change in the Baxter section of Detroit – a predominantly Jewish communtiy – was that it was the last identifiably

independent contributions of these different factors, he may have found that the ethnic composition of the population was relatively unimportant. Secondly, Tobin assumes that the attitude toward integration is a key variable influencing the move-stay decision in racially mixed communities. In fact, most empirical studies of the subject, including Chapters 4 and 5 of this volume, indicate that this is not the case. Thirdly, many of the Jews who have remained in and moved into University City in recent years have been Orthodox, and such Jews tend to have conservative attitudes toward racial integration.

Jewish community within the city boundaries. Presumably this factor provided more of an obstacle to moving among religious than non-religious families.

The tendency of religious families to remain longer in changing neighborhoods is also illustrated by the activities of the Lubavitch Hasidic sect (an ultra-orthodox Jewish group) in the Crown Heights section of Brooklyn (Kandell, 1972; Lichtenstein, 1974). During the 1960's, the community underwent racial change and most of the middle class Jewish population moved away. The Lubavitch *Rebbe* (the leader of the sect) decreed that it would be wrong for members of the sect to move away. Low interest loans have been utilized to assist Hasidic families in purchasing homes in the area. As a result of the decree and activities such as the housing loans, the area has stabilized with a black majority. It should be noted, however, that the activities of the Lubavitch Jews are somewhat atypical even among Orthodox (non-Hasidic) Jews. That is due to the particularly strong feeling of allegiance among Hasidim toward the *Rebbe*.

Among the other white ethnic groups, Italians have been noted for the stability of their neighborhoods. Furthermore, many of these neighborhoods have been able to remain healthy and solidly Italian even when surrounded by predominantly black ghetto areas. Norton Long (1977) notes that Italian Hill is one of the few remaining healthy working class communities in St. Louis. It is a community of tiny houses on tiny lots. Anywhere else in the city, a community of its income level and with its housing characteristics would be a slum. Furthermore, it has remained healthy without any governmental assistance. Similarly, Kifner (1977) notes that despite the large scale incidence of abandonment and vandalism that has plagued the Bushwick section of New York City, a healthy solidly Italian enclave remains within the community.

Gans (1962) in his study of the West End of Boston, provides one possible explanation as to why Italian communities are so stable. He notes the strong emphasis that Italians give to familial relationships, and points out that this is frequently translated into a desire among the children to live in the same neighborhood as their parents. Thus, the stability of Italian communities may be attributable to the fact that vacancies are rarely available to outsiders. They are utilized by children of families living in the community.

There is some question as to whether this explanation for stability is applicable only to Italian communities. Gans has suggested that this familial closeness is a working class rather than a specifically Italian phenomenon.

Greeley (1971) disagrees, noting that of all the ethnic groups, Italians most often live in the same neighborhood as their parents and siblings. Furthermore, these ethnic differentials persist even when variations in social class are held constant.

Researchers have noted the stability of other ethnic communities besides those inhabited by Italians. For example, Cressey (1975) indicates the tendency of Poles to remain concentrated in their original ghetto areas. The literature contains few explanations of the stability of these Eastern European communities. Researchers have, however, attempted to explain the tendency of these neighborhoods to resist black inmigration. These explanations are helpful in understanding their stability. Friedman (1971: 30) explains the resistance of Polish neighborhoods to black inmigration in the following way:

The landless Polish peasant who came to this country found his opportunity to make something of himself through the acquisition of a home, which symbolized for him the freedom, dignity and security he found in the New World. A threat to the neighborhood by the movement in of blacks is a threat to property which in turn is a threat to the core of his selfhood.

Let us assume that the stability of these communities is attributable to the attachment of immigrant families to the land. What will happen when the immigrant generation dies off? Will third and fourth generation Polish Americans have the same ties to residential properties in Polish neighborhoods without these memories? If not, the future stability of such neighborhoods will be in doubt.

2.2.2. Characteristics of the racial succession process once it begins

Efforts to resist the entry of the first black family usually fail because one or more white families has to sell out of necessity (e.g., the household head has been transferred). The first black families tend to be upwardly mobile and are attracted to the area because of the quality of the housing rather than any desire to live in an integrated community (Northwood and Barth, 1965). There has been a range of reactions to the arrival of the first black families, from violence (Rose, 1960:15; Bressler, 1960) to pressure on real estate brokers not to sell to blacks, to quiet acceptance (Northwood and Barth, 1965; Zehner and Chapin, 1974). It is widely believed that realtors play a key role in stimulating the process of racial change. In the initial stages of succession, realtors may use scare tactics (i.e., 'block busting') to encourage whites to panic move (Grier and Grier, 1966:85; Cohen, 1960:21; Wilkes, 1971; Arthur D. Little Inc., 1969:89; Chambers, 1976). Later when realtors begin to perceive that the area is 'turning', they begin to employ steering tactics, that is they show houses in the area only to blacks (Freeman and Sunshine, 1970:45; Sullivan, 1976). Existing research suggests that blockbusting and steering are not preconditions for racial transition. There have been a number of recent case studies where realtor activities have had little impact on the rate of racial change (Barresi, 1972; Molotch, 1972).

The concept of the tipping point has been widely used by laymen, practitioners and social scientists to describe the racial succession process (Northwood and Klein, 1965). Typically, this concept has been used to refer to a 'leaving' point, the maximum proportion of blacks that a neighborhood can tolerate before white residents begin to panic move (Grodzins, 1957). However, this concept has been used in at least two other ways: (1) a 'willingness to enter' point, the maximum proportion of blacks that a neighborhood can tolerate before prospective white residents begin to avoid moving into the area; and (2) the 'preference' point, the proportion of blacks considered desirable (Wolf, 1963).

In recent years social scientists have questioned the validity of the concept of the tipping point. Northwood and Klein (1965) note that although this concept is widely used by practitioners, no one definition is generally employed. In addition, it appears that, contrary to popular belief, racial change is not necessarily accompanied by white panic moving. Molotch (1972) in a study of the racially changing South Shore community (Chicago), found that the mobility rate was not higher than in comparable communities not experiencing racial change.

It is widely believed that 'in general, the process of racial transition is irreversible; once blacks start moving to certain neighborhoods, those neighborhoods tend to change from white to black' (Ginsberg, 1975:9). This assertion seems to be valid for communities adjoining black ghetto areas. There are only a handful of stable integrated communities in such situations: West Mt. Airy, Philadelphia (Guttentag, 1970); Cleveland Heights and Ludlow, Cleveland (mentioned in Aldrich, 1975); Hyde Park-Kenwood, Chicago (Farrell, 1973); Oak Park, Chicago (Williams and Simons, 1977); and University City, St. Louis (Tobin, undated). Most communities at such locations undergo complete turnover because of the pressure of black housing demand.

This does not mean that stable integration is uncommon. Bradburn *et al*.

(1971:49) estimate that approximately one out of every five American families lives in a stable integrated neighborhood. (According to the authors, stable integration occurs when a community is open to blacks and both blacks and whites are moving into the area.) Most of this integration occurs in three community contexts: (1) large scale private projects where the central management uses 'benign quotas' to maintain stability (Cohen, 1960; Millen, 1973: 156); (2) redevelopment areas in the central city consisting primarily of apartments (where the level of black housing demand is usually relatively low, (Bradburn *et al.*, 1971:25-29); and (3) suburban communities distant from existing black ghetto areas (Northwood and Barth, 1965; Bradburn *et al.*, 1971: 19-47). Furthermore, most of the integration even in these contexts is of the token variety (i.e., less than 10 percent black).

Although it is commonly believed that communities 'turn quickly', previous research has indicated that there have been considerable variations in the rate of racial transition. As Molotch (1972) notes, 'complete turnover may take several months, several years or more than a decade.'

There have been two empirical studies of factors influencing rates of racial change. On the basis of a study of patterns of transition in four Philadelphia communities Rapkin and Grigsby (1960:117) conclude:

The variations in the rate of transition are not, as commonly thought, simply a measure of differences in the intensity of prejudice and discrimination. Rather differences in rates are due to variations in all the factors analyzed... which affect the level of white demand, the level of Negro demand, the number and race of families who wish to sell their homes and the interaction of these three variables...

Rapid transition in the study areas was the product of numerous influences: liberal mortgage terms, sustained Negro demand, a substantial supply of old houses of fair quality and moderate value, rising prices, considerable activity by professional real estate operators, and a ready availability of high-quality housing for whites in other sections of the city and suburbs... By comparison slow transition in other neighborhoods was associated with a moderately large percentage of low quality housing for which financing was difficult to obtain, or of expensive housing which most Negro families could not afford.

Caplan and Wolf (1960) attempted to predict differences in the rates of racial transition between two predominantly residential areas, Russel Woods, Detroit ($^3/_4$ Jewish) and Ludlow, Cleveland ($^1/_3$ Jewish). On the basis of previous research the authors concluded that ten factors would be associated with rapid transition:

- that blacks are of relatively low socio-economic status
- that established white residents are relatively prejudiced
- that the white community is relatively transient

- the black housing market i.e., that blacks have only a limited number of options available to them in suburban areas
- that there is a relatively high degree of deterioration in housing conditions and neighborhood standards
- close proximity to black housing areas and the extent to which the community is bounded on all sides by black concentrations
- growing undesirability of the area
- realtor activities
- grass roots organizations
- the presence of a large Jewish population. 'From observations made in many large cities, the ecological pattern of invasion and succession has often been for blacks to follow Jews in housing areas. This is probably due in part to the value placed on non-violence by the Jewish community. In addition, if it is true that Jewish groups are generally more cohesive, their own tendency to self segregation might stipulate a rapid regrouping in another area as soon as invasion occurs'.

With respect to six of the ten characteristics it was anticipated that change would be more rapid in Russel Woods. With respect to four others, the communities were about equal. It was, therefore, anticipated that change would be more rapid in Russel Woods. In fact, the rates were virtually equal.

An examination of both these studies indicates that although some progress has been made in identifying the factors associated with rates of racial change, relatively little is known about the relative importance of these factors. Furthermore, the notion that Jewish communities undergo racial change more rapidly than non-Jewish ones has not been empirically verified. While this volume does not examine whether Jewish communities undergo change more rapidly than non-Jewish ones, it will look at a related question. Does a family's identification as Jewish, contribute to explaining variations in mobility in a racially changing Jewish community?

A variety of approaches has been utilized by governmental and non-governmental bodies to achieve stabilization.[2] The local residents' association has, however, been the mechanism most frequently utilized to achieve stability. Typically, resident associations focus on halting the exodus of whites, but some have concentrated on attracting a sufficient number of new white residents to the area (Wolf and Lebeaux, 1967). Resident association activities include (1) attempts to control real estate solicitation (through persuasion and through legislation); (2) maintaining and enhancing community standards (by lobbying for more community services and by working on the preparation and implementation of community master plans); and (3) building neighborhood morale and cohesion and

2. Chapter 1 contains a discussion of these approaches.

correcting stereotypes about blacks (through, for example, local block clubs).

Generally speaking, resident associations have had little impact on the rate of racial change because they have not dealt with the underlying causes of racial change (i.e., the forces responsible for black housing demand being concentrated on white communities adjoining the ghetto; Aldrich, 1975). Ironically, as Molotch (1972) points out, these efforts may even speed up the rate of transition by making the area more attractive for middle class blacks. These efforts are likely to have little impact on prospective white residents because they generally have a variety of modern suburban neighborhoods open to them.

In recent years, synagogues, Jewish Federations and Jewish Community Relations Councils have begun to play a more active role in efforts to stabilize racially changing Jewish communities. The typical approach to stabilization has been to support the creation of resident community councils. A reform congregation was instrumental in the formation of the South Shore Commission, Chicago (Molotch, 1972:68). The Mattapan Organization, Boston (Ginsberg, 1975:38) was under the sponsorship of the Jewish Community Council of Metropolitan Boston. Neither of these organizations appears to have had any appreciable impact on the rate of racial transition. In fact, most of those interviewed by Ginsberg had not heard of the Mattapan Organization.

Sklare (1971:109) has criticized the stabilization efforts of the organized Jewish community:

the federations have not moved decisively, massively, or significantly. Their problem is understandable: the effect, of the urban crisis on the Jewish householder, merchant or teacher cannot be mitigated by the old expedient of philanthropism. The only effective remedy is political rather than philanthropic – the agency must cast tradition aside and organize a power bloc that will complete with other blocs, and use its leverage with a wide variety of local, state and federal government bodies.

Sklare's comments emphasize the fact that there may be distinctive Jewish interests in racially changing communities that differ from those of other ethnic groups (e.g., blacks). For example, while Jews in a changing community may be interested in the goal of stabilization, blacks may (understandably) place a greater emphasis on the maintenance of high standards of community quality.

One of the few stabilization efforts that appears to have recognized the distinctive interests of the Jewish population in racially changing communities has been the program in Cleveland Heights supported by the Jewish

Federation of Greater Cleveland (Council of Jewish Federations and Welfare Funds, 1974:4-5). The stabilization effort includes a program of mortgage assistance aimed at attracting Jewish families. Two other facets of the stabilization effort do, however, deal with the broader (non-Jewish as well as Jewish) community:

- an intensive public relations effort directed to ease anxiety and tensions among old residents with a view of discouraging their departure;
- a human relations program designed to help in the interaction of the Jewish community with other ethnic, religious, civic and cultural organizations in the community.

At the present time it is too early to judge whether the program in Cleveland Heights has been more successful than earlier efforts.

2.2.3. Long term ecological consequences of succession

In general neighborhood racial change has a greater impact on neighborhood organizations and institutions than on the social and economic characteristics of the population (Aldrich, 1975). The following sections separately discuss these two types of impacts.

1. Socio-economic changes

Racial changes have usually had little or no impact on the socio-economic and housing characteristics of the population. During the pre-invasion stages, the more affluent whites are drawn to newer suburban areas. The available housing opportunities are usually taken by upwardly mobile black families (Bullough, 1969; Connolly, 1973; Ahlbrandt and Brophy, 1975).

Black income and educational levels have usually been found to be equal to, or in some cases, higher than those of whites in mixed areas (Aldrich, 1975:339; Taeuber and Taeuber, 1965:164; Duncan and Duncan, 1957; Wolf and Lebeaux, 1969; Ginsberg, 1975:158). This generalization requires three qualifications. Firstly, racial changes have been often accompanied by declines in occupational prestige levels (Molotch, 1972:76). Blacks tend to be concentrated in blue collar occupations, while whites are concentrated in white collar jobs (Arthur D. Little Inc., 1969:36; Taeuber and Taeuber, 1965:159). Secondly, black families are more likely to have multiple earners. Thirdly, the inmigration of even a small number of poor black families may have a serious negative impact on a community. In his study of the South Shore community of Chicago, Molotch (1972:99) found that black inmigrants were generally in the middle income categories, but there was a small but significant number of poor black inmigrants. As a result, racial transition was accompanied by an increase in the incidence of welfare. The importance of this increase was magnified by white residents, because prior to black inmigration, it was virtually unknown for community residents to receive welfare.

Contrary to the fears of white residents, racial changes have usually not altered the proportion of homeowners. The Taeubers (1965:165) note that owner occupancy is the major vehicle for the entry of blacks into mixed areas, and that blacks in invasion tracts are more likely than whites to be homeowners. The Duncans (1957) assert that blacks seek homeownership in mixed areas in order to avoid exorbitant rents within the ghetto.

One of the weaknesses of previous research on black-white differences in changing neighborhoods is that they have not compared whites and blacks of similar types (e.g., at the same stage of the family life cycle). One would suspect that the degree of resemblance in income and education noted in previous studies is partially attributable to differences between the two populations in age structure (i.e., the fact that the white population is older). This would suggest that if whites and blacks of the same age or position in family life cycle were compared, wider differences would emerge. Unfortunately, it has not been possible to make this type of comparison in previous studies due to their almost exclusive reliance on federal census data which present black-white comparisons on only one characteristic at a time. One of the aims of this volume is to make the types of detailed comparisons mentioned above utilizing the results of the telephone survey of Wynnefield residents.

2. Impacts on community standards

a. Schools

Racial changes have had a particularly sharp impact on the student bodies of schools serving transitional communities. Typically, these changes have occurred more rapidly in the schools than in the surrounding communities (Molotch, 1972:131-47; Wolf and Lebeaux, 1969; Bradburn et al., 1971:141; Ginsberg, 1975:48-50). Three factors have been mentioned in the literature as accounting for this pattern. Firstly, schools in these areas (particularly junior and senior high schools) tend to draw from a wider area which would include predominantly black communities in the inner city.

Secondly, white couples with young children tend to be among the first to move from transitional communities. Finally, families that can afford to, send their children to private or parochial schools.

Often, changes in the racial composition of school populations have been accompanied by changes in school variables (e.g., increases in overcrowding, increases in the rate of faculty turnover, etc.). Existing research suggests that white parents are usually more concerned about changes in the social composition of the student body than they are about changes in school variables (Molotch, 1972:92). The reluctance of white parents to keep their children in racially changing schools is partly due to the fact that blacks are usually viewed as a distinct cultural group, and white parents are unwilling to have their children be part of a racial minority (Downs, 1968, Bradburn et al., 1971:145; Ravitz, 1957). Another factor contributing to this reluctance on the part of white parents is the perception that racial changes are accompanied by changes in the social class backgrounds of the students (Wolf and Lebeaux, 1967:108).

> Racial changes in occupancy involves shifts in the social class proportions of an area more often than is commonly realized... In many instances, a substantial proportion of the entering Negro households will be 'respectable working class' – often with both husband and wife employed. Especially if the area (as has often been the case) was formerly occupied to a large extent by Jewish households, the difference in average school performance may be noticeable. If these changes are accompanied by even small increases in the proportion of pupils who are rowdy, physically aggressive, or otherwise threatening to middle-class standards of language and other behavior, former residents may decide to leave.

Tobin (undated) emphasizes the importance of the schools in achieving stable integration in his study of University City, Missouri (a suburb of St. Louis). In recent years, University City has achieved 'some measure of integration' despite continued black inmigration. The schools have been a different story, however. Overall, 65 percent of the students in the city schools were black and 4 of the 8 elementary schools were 90 percent or more black. Tobin notes (p. 13):

> Schools are crucial as an indicator of the racial and social mix of an area, and as an attraction for young families with children to add stability. An overwhelming number of blacks in the schools could become a deterrent in attracting whites who determine the degree of integration of the area. The schools could be the 'tipping mechanism in University City.'

A final type of research relevant to this question is that dealing with the relationship between school desegregation and white flight. James Coleman (1973, 1977) has found a relationship between the implementation of mandatory busing and white flight. Racially mixed neighborhoods on the edge of the ghetto are often the ones most seriously affected by such policies since they contain some of the limited number of white children remaining in the central city. Coleman's research implies that changes in the racial composition of the schools in these neighborhoods (possibly resulting from the busing in of black children from the inner city) contributes to the decisions to move among white parents with children in the public schools.

A journalistic account, related to Los Angeles (Lindsey, 1977) makes the same point, i.e., that mandatory busing was leading to an exodus of whites from the school district. Dr. David Armor and Dr. Howard Freeman, U.C.L.A., estimated (on the basis of a survey) that 35,000 families would withdraw from the Los Angeles school district if mandatory busing were implemented. Reynolds Farley (1975, 1977) had originally criticized Coleman's findings and had argued that no relationship existed between desegregation and white flight. More recently, he has revised his conclusions finding that such a relationship existed (Fiske, 1977).

b. *Housing*
Racial succession has frequently been accompanied by deterioration of the housing stock, leading to unusually high rates of abandonment (HUD, 1973:5; Sternlieb *et al.*, 1974; Ginsberg, 1975: ix). During the early stages of transition, housing deterioration is attributable to the changing age composition of the population rather than to racial changes per se. At the time of black entry, housing is typically at the threshold of accelerated decay. 'The acquisition of housing already going downhill by families that are younger and larger than those of previous occupants, hastens the process that was previously less perceptible' (Rose, 1969:210). During later stages of the succession process, three forces specifically related to racial change promote deterioration. Firstly, it is fairly common for landlords to decrease maintenance as the proportion of blacks in the community increases (Molotch, 1972: 16; HUD, 1973: 51-53). The decision to decrease maintenance levels may be related to the belief that newer black tenants will not be as concerned with the upkeep of their apartments or it may be based on a generally pessimistic assessment of the future of the community. More specifically, this pessimism may be based on the belief that income levels will go down and that as a result, it will not be possible to set rents at a high enough level to meet costs (Ahlbrandt and Brophy, 1975). Secondly, vandalism, both by tenants and non-tenants, including youth gangs, seems to be due, in part, to racial antagonism between tenants and

landlords and increasing abdication of management responsibility by landlords (HUD, 1973: 67). Thirdly, banks have traditionally 'redlined' transitional communities, and it has been difficult for residents to obtain home improvements as well as mortgage loans.[3] Housing deterioration is not, however, an inevitable consequence of transition. There are communities which have undergone complete transition from white to black and remain physically attractive and well maintained. Three factors serve as barriers to abandonment in communities experiencing racial transition: (1) a substantial black middle class; (2) a high rate of ownership; and (3) a tight housing market for middle class blacks, which tends to hold them to the area (HUD, 1973: 78).

c. *Property values*

The notion that racial change is accompanied by declines in property values is without substantiation.[4] As noted by Abrams (1966: 64-76), there has been no single price reaction to increases in black occupancy; in some cases, prices have increased and in others they have declined (see also Laurenti, 1960: 52-3; Millen, 1973; Ginsberg, 1975: 168). Price declines may occur if black demand is insufficient to absorb all of the vacancies made available by white outmigration (Rose, 1970; Freeman and Sunshine, 1970: 49). Where price declines do occur, they may actually improve the prospects for

3. 'Redlining is the refusal by lending institutions to make mortgage or home improvement loans in areas that the institutions deem risks even though they may have never lost money in these areas' (Farrell, 1975). This practice has a severe impact on racially changing communities. An area shunned by lenders will soon decline for lack of funds necessary for upkeep. In recent years, there have been a number of reports documenting the existence of this practice, e.g., in New York (Fowler, 1977) and in Washington, D.C. (Cerra, 1976). There is considerable debate as to whether redlining is a cause or a result of neighborhood succession. Critics charge that the banks' decisions, as to whether to provide loans, are shortsighted in that they do not take into account the impacts on communities, and are unrelated to the actual risks involved. On the other hand, 'bankers say they are scapegoats to the fundamental forces affecting these neighborhoods. They cite the departure of middle class families and their replacement by poorer families. Further they emphasize that their primary responsibility is to invest their depositors money prudently' (Fried, 1977).
4. Laurenti's study has been extensively cited by other researchers to support the argument that racial changes do not increase the probability of declines in property values. However, due to limitations in his methodology, Laurenti's work may be of only limited value to racially changing communities (Downs, 1973). Laurenti examined neighborhoods in three cities: Philadelphia, San Francisco and Oakland. Test neighborhoods where black inmigration had occurred were compared with control neighborhoods that had remained predominantly white during this period. A key point is that most of the test neighborhoods were some distance from the boundaries of existing ghetto areas. Therefore, the findings may not be applicable to other racially changing communities along the edge of the ghetto.

racial stability. Guttentag (1970) notes that price declines, following the initial entry of blacks into the West Mt. Airy section of Philadelphia, helped to attract middle class whites. The prices after the declines were still out of the range of a substantial proportion of blacks in the inner city, and thus black housing demand was not concentrated in this area.

d. *Street crime*

Violent street crime has been one of the most serious concerns of residents of racially changing communities. Molotch, in his study of the South Shore community in Chicago (1972) found that residents' perceptions – that racial change was accompanied by increased crime – were supported by existing data. That is, there was an increase in street crime, as indicated by arrest rates, increases in police beats and increases in the utilization of the emergency room of the local hospital.

That the crime problem is a real one for residents is shown by the results of Ginsberg's study of the Mattapan section of Boston (1975). Thirty nine out of the 100 interviewed had been victimized. The crime problem created a climate of fear in the community. Residents tended to avoid side streets and they avoided shopping during certain hours when teenagers were likely to be out.

The problem of street crime has certainly not been limited to racially changing Jewish communities, such as the South Shore community in Chicago or the Mattapan section of Boston. Bradburn *et al.*, (1971: 173-4) found that in a nationwide sample residents and informants (i.e., community leaders) in integrated neighborhoods were more concerned about street crime than residents and informants in white segregated neighborhoods. Furthermore, street crime, accompanying racial shifts, has sharply altered the life styles in non-Jewish white ethnic neighborhoods – as is indicated by this quote from a neighborhood priest in the racially changing East Side of Cleveland (Wilkes, 1971:10).

Novenas and other night-time services have been stopped. The old ladies of the church were getting beaten and robbed on their way to early mass, so we stopped those...We had a lot of trouble with school children being beaten, in fact the entire baseball team and their coaches were overrun by a gang of 30...

White and black residents of transitional communities often differ in the way they evaluate the seriousness of existing crime (Wilkes, 1971). While white residents often view their community as crime ridden, newer black residents view the same community as crime free. This seeming discrepancy is due to the fact that whites compare the current community with what it was before racial change began (when street crime may have been a rarity) or to suburban areas (where their friends or relatives may live), whereas blacks compare the current incidence of crime with that in the inner city neighborhood from which they moved (where the incidence of crime is usually quite high).

There has been a lack of consensus among researchers regarding the impact of the problem of street crime on moving decisions. Gordon (1959:10-11) asserts that fear for personal safety has been one of the most important factors leading to the migration of Jews from central city to suburban areas throughout the United States. Wilkes (1971) suggests that the security problem was one of the most important underlying causes of transition in the East Side of Cleveland. On the other hand, the nationwide survey cited above (Bradburn *et al.*, 1971:175), revealed that 'crime does not influence many moving decisions' (in integrated neighborhoods). Furthermore, Droettboom *et al.* (1971) based on a nationwide survey of residents living in *all* types of neighborhoods in metropolitan areas, found that perceptions of neighborhood crime and violence had little relationship to significant extra-neighborhood changes in residential locations.[5]

2.3. The household migration decision

2.3.1. Models of the mobility decision

While ecological studies are useful for describing past population movements, the ecological approach has been far less helpful in either explaining these movements or in predicting future movements. These inadequacies are related to three criticisms directed toward ecological explanations of migration. First, ecologists place too heavy a reliance on the analogy between the behavior of social groups and plant and animal patterns

---

5. Droettboom *et al.* had hypothesized that if families were seriously affected by crime, they would move outside the neighborhood. This is why only moves outside the neighborhood were used in support of the hypothesis that crime influenced mobility. This may not be a valid assumption. Some families may move within a neighborhood – from a single family home to a high rise apartment – in order to obtain a greater sense of security. It therefore can be argued that Droettboom should not have distinguished between intra- and extra-neighborhood moves in examining this relationship. Had both of these types of moves been combined, it is likely that a significant relationship would have resulted.

without giving adequate attention to the basis for the analogies. Secondly, a lack of attention is given to psychological motivations, and the social structuring of these motivations, in explaining how individual families actually make the move-stay decision. Finally, ecology has been criticized for the reliance placed on the aggregative principle in which it is assumed that the behavior of the group can be described as the sum of individual actions (Beshers, 1962:13-34; Gettys, 1966: 98-103). There is increasing consensus among social scientists that in order to understand population shifts, it is necessary to focus on the mobility decisions of individual households.

A number of conceptual models of the household migration decision have been developed in recent years (Butler et al., 1971; Wolpert, 1965). These efforts have been synthesized in a recent review article by Moore (1972). The household migration decision is divided into two separate decisions: (1) the decision to seek a new residence; and (2) the search for and selection of a new residence. (Our primary interest in this volume is in the first decision.) Figure 1 is Moore's conceptual model of the decision to seek a new residence. As shown, this decision is influenced by the household head's evaluation of the current location (i.e., the dwelling unit and the surrounding neighborhood). Among the factors influencing this evaluation is the social composition of the neighborhood. As Moore (1972:8) indicates: 'Complaints about the social composition of the neighborhood arise in two ways: either the neighborhood is undergoing some change which the individual deems undesirable or the individual's expectations regarding his social environment change.'

There have been two basic approaches to explaining the impact of neighborhood racial changes on family decision making: (1) studies of the manifest causal relationships; and (2) studies of the latent causal relationships. In the former approach, respondents are asked for their reasons for moving, or alternatively are asked whether specific factors were important in their decisions to move. The advantage of this approach is its directness. However, as Kadushin (1968:342) notes: 'actors may not know the "real" reasons for their actions and the researcher may be collecting a set of mere rationalizations'. Research on the manifest causal relationships has emphasized three concerns – dealing with crime, public schools and property values – in explaining the residential mobility decisions of white families in racially changing communities. (We have already discussed these three concerns in connection with our discussion of the impacts of racial change on community standards.)

The preceding suggests that it is important for researchers to look at the latent causal relationships involved in migration. In studying these relationships which are involved in migration, researchers seek to predict on the basis of theory or theories, which types of families are most likely to move in given situations. This volume utilizes both of the above two approaches in order to explain the underlying causes of mobility decisions among Wynnefield residents. Chapters 4 and 5 test for the importance of different demographic and attitudinal variables in predicting moving plans and moving behavior among Wynnefield residents. Chapter 6 examines the perceived reasons for moving among Wynnefield residents.

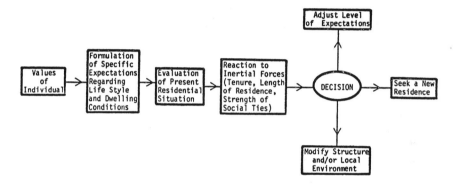

Figure 1.   Elements affecting the decision to seek a new residence.

Source: Moore, 1972: 5.

In discussing the personality characteristics that influence mobility decisions in racially changing communities the following section distinguishes between two types of variables: (1) those that affect the susceptibility of white families generally; and (2) those that influence the susceptibility of Jewish families in particular.

1. Personality characteristics affecting the mobility decisions of white families in general

a. *Racial prejudice*
It has frequently been assumed both by laymen and social scientists, that

prejudiced individuals are the first to move from racially changing neighborhoods (Freeman and Sunshine, 1970; Sabagh *et al.*, 1969). Prejudice has been defined as an attitude of favor or disfavor and an overgeneralized belief toward members of another group (Allport, 1958: 12-13). When the association between prejudice and outmigration decisions has been tested, insignificant results have usually been obtained. Mayer (cited in Taeuber and Taeuber, 1965: 173) found that the degree of prejudice was not a reliable indicator of who actually moved during the course of transition in the Russel Woods section of Detroit. Bradburn *et al.*, (1971: 124) based on a nationwide survey of integrated neighborhoods, make a more general statement: 'residential choice (i.e., whether to move into or away from a racially changing community) is relatively independent of attitudes... whatever one's preference for integrated or segregated living is secondary to the more important question of where one can get the best apartment or house within one's financial means.'

The fact that the level of racial prejudice is not an accurate predictor of behavior is understandable in the context of studies showing that racial prejudice does not necessarily lead to discriminatory or avoidance behavior toward blacks. Berelson and Steiner (1964: 505) note that there are numerous occasions where discrimination occurs without prejudice, and prejudice without discrimination. Merton (in McEntire, 1960: 81) sets up a two dimensional classification of the population based on the levels of prejudice and discrimination. He indicates that the 'unprejudiced discriminator' probably constitutes a large proportion of the population. Allport (1958: 14-15) indicates that there are degrees of negative action which may arise from prejudice. Some of the alternatives mentioned by Allport are relevant to the household head in a racially mixed area. He may avoid members of the disliked group by moving away or by avoiding social contact while remaining in the area. He may remain in the area and discriminate against inmigrants by excluding them from certain privileges (e.g., prevent them from joining the local civic association or fraternal organization). Finally, he may physically attack newcomers – a situation which has often occurred in the last few years in white ethnic neighborhoods throughout the United States.

b. *Current neighborhood racial composition*
It is also widely believed that white mobility decisions are influenced by residents' perceptions of the neighborhood's current racial composition. This is reflected in the commonly accepted assumption that once the

proportion of blacks exceeds a certain point (i.e., the 'tipping point') white residents will begin to panic move. (See the section above which deals specifically with the concept of the tipping point.)

While evidence in support of the tipping point concept is limited, previous research does indicate that as the proportion of blacks in a community increases, there is a sharp, but steady drop in the demand for housing in the area by prospective white residents. A recent nationwide survey of integrated neighborhoods (Bradburn *et al.*, 1971: 61) concluded:

Of whites in any kind of integrated neighborhood, slightly less than 1 percent live in neighborhoods that are more than 50 percent Negro...
At present then it would appear that the percentage of Negroes in the neighborhood is an important variable influencing the housing choice of whites.

This would strongly imply that the perception of the proportion of blacks would be an important variable influencing the move-stay decision of white householders.

Downs (1968: 1338-9) has provided a useful explanation for the reluctance of whites to move into or remain in substantially integrated communities in terms of the 'Law of Dominance.'

...whites... want to be sure that the social, cultural, and economic millieu and values of their own group dominate their own residential environment and the educational environment of their children... The best way to insure that this will happen is to isolate somewhat oneself and one's children in an everyday environment dominated by – but not necessarily exclusively comprised of – other families and children whose social, economic, cultural and even religious views and attitudes are approximately the same as one's own... a majority of middle class white Americans still perceive race and color as relevant factors in their assessment of the kind of homogeneity they seek to attain... Therefore, in deciding whether a given neighborhood or a given school exhibits the kind of environment in which 'their own' traits are and will remain dominant, they consider Negroes as members of 'another' group.

c. *Future racial changes*

Recent studies have emphasized the importance of expectations of future racial change (rather than perceptions of the neighborhood's current racial composition) in influencing white mobility decisions (Wolf, 1957, 1963). Whites may decide to move early in the transition process (when the proportion of blacks is relatively small), if they anticipate that their neighborhood will eventually become predominantly black. It is often believed that these expectations are irrational; but, in fact, researchers have found that residents formulate these expectations on the basis of realistic assessments of the market forces impinging on their communities (Bradburn *et al.*, 1971; McEntire, 1960: 83; Wolf, 1957). That is, they are most likely to fear complete transition when their community is immediately adjacent to a predominantly black area.

While a number of researchers have discussed the above three personality characteristics, there have been few empirical studies which have compared the three in terms of their ability to explain mobility behavior. This will be one of the major aims of this volume.

d. *Future income changes*

Other researchers have suggested that changes in the social composition of the population (including changes in income levels) are as important, and possibly more important, than racial changes per se in influencing the move-stay decision. Changes in the social class composition of the population may have a serious impact on informal relationships. Homogeneity of values among neighbors is a prerequisite for friendship formation. 'Excessive heterogeneity can lead to coolness between neighbors' (Gans, 1961: 176).

Levittown, New York and Islington, London illustrate the problems of maintaining a class mixture, even when racial differences are not present. Levittown, when first settled after World War II, was a homogenous white middle class area. Inmigration of white working class families into the area led to serious controversies over school budgets (with working class families much less interested in educational innovations which might increase the size of the school budget). Dobriner (1962) predicted that if the schism between working and middle class families continued, the exodus of middle class families from Levittown would accelerate.

Islington is a working class community in London which has experienced an inmigration of middle class families who have rehabilitated older homes and who have pressured for improved city services (Hershey, 1977). This process of 'gentrification' has been resisted by working class families because it has pushed the costs of housing beyond the financial means of their children and because tax monies are perceived to be used for frills (e.g., the closing off of streets to automobile traffic).

Earlier in this chapter, we pointed out that black inmigrants to racially mixed areas usually have incomes equal to, or exceeding those of long term residents. Why is it, then, that whites often expect racial changes to be accompanied by changes in the socio-economic composition of the population? One explanation provided by Brown (1972) is that whites cannot distinguish between classes of blacks. Similarly, Pettigrew (1973) notes that whites generally believe blacks to be of low social status. It is possible, however, that white residents are aware that in the initial stages of the succession process, blacks have middle incomes. They may fear that these middle income families will be followed by lower income ones.

2.4. Personality characteristics affecting the mobility decisions of members of different white ethnic groups

Earlier in this chapter, we noted that there has been some evidence of differences among various types of white ethnic communities in their susceptibility to racial change and there has been some speculation as to the reasons for these differences. There has, however, been little research on the role of ethnic and cultural variables in the move-stay decision of *individual families* in such communities. This volume will attempt to close this gap in existing research by focusing on the importance of Jewish cultural characteristics in influencing the move-stay decision in a racially changing Jewish community. Chapter 4 will test whether the family's iden-tification as Jewish contributes to explaining variations in moving plans among Jewish and non-Jewish Wynnefield residents. We will also examine the extent to which Jewish denominational affiliation (i.e., whether the family is Orthodox, Conservative, or Reform) and frequency of synagogue attendance contribute toward explaining variations in mobility plans among Jewish residents of Wynnefield. In Chapter 5, we will test for the importance of different Jewish attitudinal and behavioral characteristics (e.g., the attitude toward driving on the Sabbath) – as compared to other race related attitudes and other background characteristics – in explaining variations in mobility behavior among Wynnefield Jews.

3. The racial transition process: Is Wynnefield a typical changing community?

3.1. Introduction

Wynnefield has undergone ethnic succession twice during this century. During the 1920's, the community shifted from predominantly white Anglo-Saxon Protestant to Eastern European Jewish. During the 1960's, the community underwent racial turnover and by 1970 the community was roughly one-half black. This chapter focuses on the latter shift. It seeks to determine the extent of resemblance between the racial transition process in Wynnefield and the process in other middle-class communities that have been studied. It also attempts to identify those aspects of the process that are distinctive to Jewish communities.

In this chapter, we will attempt to answer the following three sets of questions: Firstly, what factors made Wynnefield susceptible to racial change? To what extent did the community's ethnic composition (i.e., the fact that it was predominantly Jewish) affect its susceptibility? Secondly, how did the community react to black inmigration? What programs were implemented to achieve stable integration? How active a role did the organized Jewish community play in stabilization efforts? What impact did these efforts have on the rate of racial change? Finally, what were the long-term ecological consequences of racial succession? That is, what were the impacts of racial change on the socio-economic characteristics of the population and on community standards (e.g., changes in the quality of the local public schools)? To what extent did black and white families differ with respect to socio-economic and housing characteristics?

3.2. History of ethnic changes in Wynnefield

3.2.1. The development of Wynnefield as a Jewish enclave

Wynnefield was first settled in 1690 by Dr. Thomas Wynne, a colonial physician, who built a farm in what is known as the Upper Hill section. The development of Philadelphia began to extend toward Wynnefield during the late 1800's, spurred on by the Centennial celebration. By this time, there were clusters of large single-family homes in the Upper Hill section of the community, occupied by white Protestant families. Prior to 1920, additional single-family, and some semi-detached dwellings, were also built in Upper Wynnefield.

The most extensive development of the community occurred during the 1920's and 1930's. During the mid-twenties, developers sensed the value of the community for upwardly mobile immigrant families, and most of Lower Wynnefield was subdivided for row houses. The majority of those attracted to the area were Eastern European Jews who relocated from South Philadelphia (the city's original East European Jewish ghetto area). Soon, more well-to-do Jews began to settle in Upper Wynnefield. Ethnic change quickened as white Protestants moved away from the area. Those Protestants who remained, clustered in one section of Upper Wynnefield. A Catholic parish was established during the 1920's, with the expectation that there would be large numbers of Catholics, but relatively few moved into the community.

By 1929, Wynnefield was acknowledged as an Anglo-Jewish dormitory community (with some Catholics and Protestants) with its social life centered around a variety of religious, cultural and fraternal organizations. Several large synagogues were constructed. In addition, there were many smaller congregations which met in private homes. Up until World War II, Wynnefield was viewed (by residents and outsiders), as a prestigious suburban type community. The community's advantages included its fine schools, proximity to a large park, and rapid accessibility to downtown Philadelphia by either commuter railroad or a combination of bus and elevated subway.

3.2.2. Wynnefield becomes ripe for racial change

The image of Wynnefield began to change prior to World War II. Before this period, some upwardly mobile Jewish families had desired to move to even more prestigious communities (including those in Lower Merion Township), but had been prevented from doing so by discriminatory housing practices. When these discriminatory practices broke down, the rate of outmigration of Jewish families to these areas increased. Children of the original Jewish residents of Wynnefield tended not to remain in the community, but, instead relocated to newer Jewish enclaves which were developing in other sections of the city. This tendency to move away from

Wynnefield was attributable to two factors. Some of the children preferred not to live near their parents, while others considered the older homes in the community unfashionable. However, Wynnefield continued to attract Jewish residents during the 1950's and 1960's, and consequently maintained its image as a Jewish enclave. Although the community's religious composition did not change between 1940 and 1960, there was an upward shift in the community's age structure. The proportion 65 and over increased from 6 percent in 1940 to 8 percent in 1950 to 13 percent in 1960.[1] During the 1950's and early 1960's, West Philadelphia's black ghetto expanded in the direction of Wynnefield (Figures 1 and 2). Change in Wynnefield's all-white character seemed inevitable.[2]

3.2.3. The community undergoes racial change: the 1960's

The first black family moved into Wynnefield proper in 1963, purchasing a home from a federal agency as a result of a foreclosure. The first black families clustered in a few blocks in Lower Wynnefield, but later, blacks purchased homes throughout the community. The mid-1960's were characterized by a fairly rapid increase in the proportion of homes purchased by blacks from 8 percent in 1963 to 67 percent in the first 5 months of 1966 (Jewish Community Relations Council of Philadelphia, undated). The rate of racial change was most rapid in the Lower Hill section. On twelve blocks where substantial numbers of blacks had moved, there were no subsequent sales to whites.[3]

As the proportion of blacks increased during the mid-1960's, many white residents feared that the community would undergo rapid racial turnover and that there would be a decline in neighborhood standards (e.g., a decline

1. Unless otherwise noted, the findings presented in this chapter are from the federal census.
2. There were blacks living in Wynnefield prior to 1960. The 1960 federal census indicated the community was 4 percent non-white (Table 1 and Figure 3). However, almost all of the blacks were concentrated in the southern tip of census tract 119, in a neighborhood which was separated from the rest of the community by a major east-west artery (Lancaster Avenue). Since most residents did not consider this neighborhood part of Wynnefield, it is fair to say that Wynnefield was nearly an all-white community until 1963.
In Figure 3, letters have been used to designate the census tracts as follows: 117 = A, 120 = B, 121 = C, 119 = D, 118 = E.
3. On the basis of previous research, one would expect that a disproportionately large number of black families would have come from adjoining sections of the West Philadelphia ghetto. The 1969 telephone survey supports this expectation. West Philadelphia was the most frequently mentioned previous location among black families, being cited by three fifths (59 percent, 51) of the respondents.

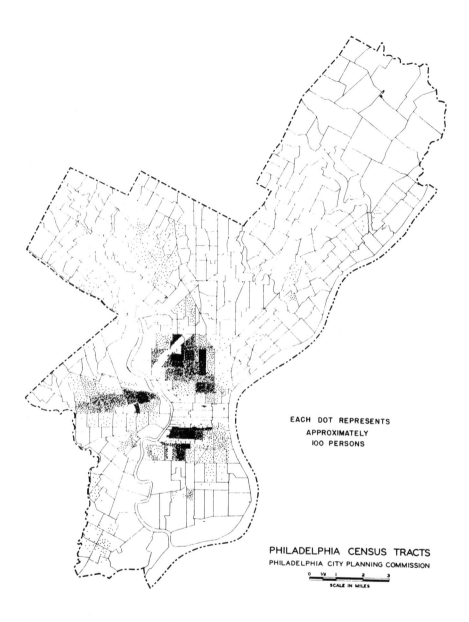

EACH DOT REPRESENTS
APPROXIMATELY
100 PERSONS

PHILADELPHIA CENSUS TRACTS
PHILADELPHIA CITY PLANNING COMMISSION

0   ½   1   2   3
SCALE IN MILES

Figure 1. Distribution of non-white population 1950.

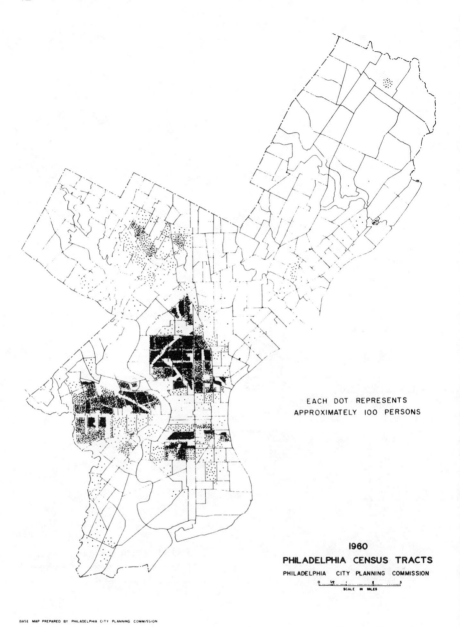

EACH DOT REPRESENTS
APPROXIMATELY 100 PERSONS

1960
PHILADELPHIA CENSUS TRACTS
PHILADELPHIA   CITY   PLANNING   COMMISSION

BASE MAP PREPARED BY PHILADELPHIA CITY PLANNING COMMISSION

Figure 2. Distribution of non-white population 1960.

Table 1. Racial changes in Wynnefield, 1960-1970.

Census tract	Total pop.		White pop.		Black pop.		Other pop.		Percent non-white	
	1960	1970	1960	1970	1960	1970	1960	1970	1960	1970
117	1491	1697	1486	1258	5	425	0	14	0.3	25.9
120	2043	2485	2024	2151	19	302	0	32	0.9	13.4
121	3327	3306	3308	3026	19	256	0	24	0.6	8.5
Upper Wynnefield (tracts 117+120+121)	6861	7488	6818	6435	43	983	0	70	0.6	14.1
119	6712	7161	5907	2140	803	4967	2	54	12.1	70.1
118	7155	7770	7145	2418	10	5280	0	72	0.1	68.9
Lower Wynnefield (tracts 119+118)	13867	14931	13052	4558	813	10247	2	126	4.1	69.5
Total	20728	22419	19870	10993	856	11230	2	176	4.1	51.0

Source: Federal census, 1960 and 1970.

in property values, a decline in the quality of schools, etc.). The Wynnefield Development Council (an umbrella body of civic and religious organizations), sought the help of the Jewish Community Relations Council of Philadelphia in order to determine whether there was any basis for these fears. The JCRC conducted a two-faceted study of the community: (1) an analysis of property transfers between 1963 and mid-1966 with respect to the racial characteristics of buyers and sellers and the prices that the homes sold for; and (2) a survey on the impact of racial changes, which was administered to a relatively small group of residents and workers in the community (e.g., real estate agents, businessmen, school principals, police officials). The report concluded that racial changes were not occurring at an alarming rate and that racial changes were not having an adverse effect on community life.

...racial changes taking place in the area are not drastic, have not depreciated property values, quality of public school education and have not in any way impaired the neighborhood (Jewish Community Relations Council of Philadelphia, undated: 10).[4]

4. Later sections of this chapter show that these conclusions were unrealistically optimistic in light of the actual rate and character of racial changes in the community during the 1960's.

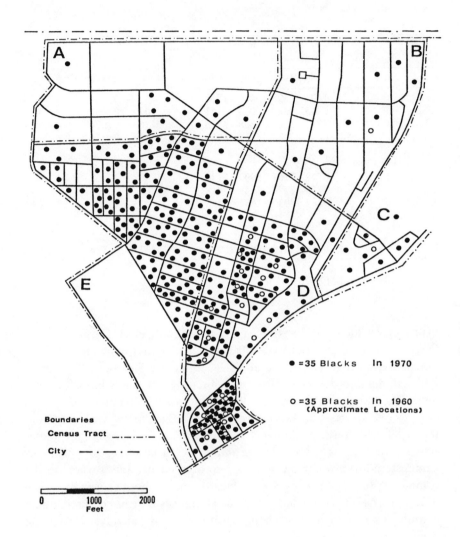

Figure 3. Blacks.

The Wynnefield Residents Association was founded in 1957 around the proposed location of a firehouse in the community. The desire of whites to maintain a stable integrated community may have provided the impetus for the growth of the Association during the early 1960's. Nevertheless, the stated goal was to improve the quality of life for all residents rather than to promote racial stability.

Our goals are to improve educational facilities, to press for needed city services, to exclude objectionable uses (such as bars) and to develop a community spirit of participation in the solution of community problems (*Newsletter,* November, 1969).[5]

The Residents Association has become involved in a wide variety of activities and programs aimed at improving the community: organizing social and recreational activities (e.g., banquets, track meets); organizing block clubs throughout the community; lobbying for improvement in city services and in neighborhood maintenance; distributing health information; helping to organize security patrols for crime protection; publishing a bi-weekly newsletter with a circulation of 5,000; participating (through its Zoning Committee) in all matters affecting changes in land use in the community; and participating (along with the Area Planner from the City Planning Commission) in the preparation of a long-range master plan for the community. In order to control real estate solicitation, the Association has obtained voluntary agreement from local realtors to limit the level of telephone and mail canvassing.

The growth of the Wynnefield Residents Association during the late 1960's and early 1970's is reflected in the organization's budget data (Table 2). Between 1967 and 1974 the Residents Association's income increased six-fold (426 percent) from $2,092 to $12,463. The organized Jewish community provided a limited amount of financial assistance to the organization. During the 1968-9 fiscal year, the Philadelphia Federation of Jewish Agencies allocated $2,500; while during the 1973-4 fiscal year, the Jewish Community Relations Council allocated $1,500.

The activities of the Wynnefield Residents Association and the Jewish Community Relations Council do not appear to have affected the rate of

5. The goal of stable integration is not mentioned in any issue of the Association newsletter. Molotch (1972: Chapter 4) notes a similar tendency (i.e., to avoid race related issues) in the statements and publications of the South Shore Commission (Chicago). Commission statements did not mention racial integration as a goal, but such phrases as a good community and a good place to live. These were interpreted by whites as meaning the maintenance of the community's white middle class character.

Table 2. Income and expenses of the Wynnefield Residents Association 1967 to 1974.

Year	Income	Expenses
1967	$ 2,092	$ 1,793
1968	3,769	2,086
1969	n.a.	n.a.
1970	n.a.	n.a.
1971	6,261	6,895
1972	8,791	7,900
1973	8,819	10,488
1974	12,463	10,606

n.a. = not available.

Source: Wynnefield Residents Association.

racial change. At the time of the 1969 telephone survey, blacks comprised about one third (31 percent, 647) of the total population surveyed.[6] Jews still comprised the largest ethnic group, with about one half (55 percent) of the total. There were smaller numbers of white Catholics (10 percent) and white Protestants (4 percent). Figure 4 portrays the spatial distribution of members of the three religious groups in the study area in 1969. In examining this map the reader should keep in mind the fact that most (85 percent) of the Protestants surveyed in Wynnefield are black.

By 1970, the community was a demographically biracial one (i.e., about 50 percent black, see Table 1). As shown in Figure 3, there were sharp differences in the rates of racial transition within the community. Whereas Lower Wynnefield had become a predominantly black area by 1970 (70 percent black), Upper Wynnefield remained predominantly white. The Jewish Community Relations Council report, mentioned above, suggested that there were two principal reasons for the rapid rate of transition in Lower Wynnefield (p. 14): (1) concentrated campaigns in those blocks by real estate operators to sell; and (2) the price range of homes in these particular streets was lower than elsewhere in Wynnefield and these homes could, therefore, be better afforded by black purchasers. Later, the report also indicated (p. 17) that the relative stability of the Upper Hill section was

6. Unlike the other results from the telephone survey discussed in this chapter, these refer to individuals rather than families. These findings were obtained by multiplying the number of families in the four ethnic groups by the mean family size for each group.

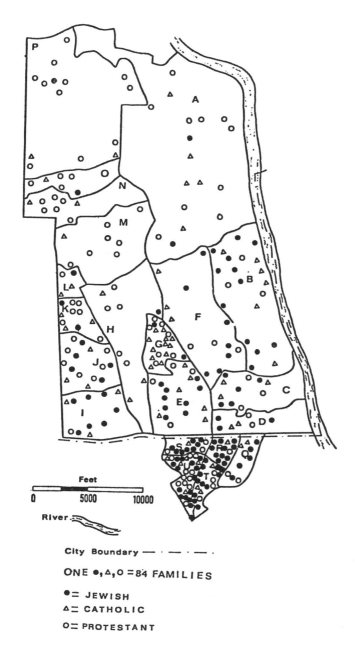

Figure 4. Distribution of religious groups.

attributable to the fact that the homes and streets were particularly attractive and because the higher priced homes represented particular values
as compared to what was available elsewhere in Philadelphia.

3.3. Long term ecological consequences of succession

3.3.1. Shifts in the demographic composition of the population

1. Life cycle characteristics
Previous studies have indicated that racial change generally involves the
replacement of middle age and elderly white families without children by
younger black families with children. As a result, racial change has typically
been accompanied by a lowering of the average age level. The results for
Wynnefield generally parallel this earlier research.

Table 3 and Figure 5 show that as of 1970 blacks were disproportionately
represented among children and young adults while whites were disproportionately represented among the elderly. Furthermore, the average
family size of blacks was considerably higher than that for whites. Similarly,
Table 4 (utilizing the telephone survey results) indicates that a disproportionately large number of black families were young and with children while
a disproportionately large number of the white families were middle aged
and elderly couples (or individuals) without children at home.

Given the above findings – the replacement of older whites by younger
blacks – it is not at all surprising that Wynnefield experienced a radical
downward shift in the age structure during the 1960's (Table 5), with a
decline in the median age from 41.3 to 37.0 years. Between 1960 and 1970,
there was a substantial increase in the proportion of children under 10 years
(from 5 to 8 percent), and relatively young adults, 20 to 44 years (from 26 to
33 percent), but a sharp decrease in the proportion of residents in their
middle years, 45 to 64 (from 36 to 22 percent). There was, however, no
appreciable change in the proportion of elderly persons, above 65 (from
13.8 to 14.1 percent).

Given the above results dealing with age shifts, one would expect that
there would have been an increase in the mean family size during the
1960's. It is, therefore, somewhat surprising that during this period, there
was a slight decline in the average family size, from 3.0 in 1960 to 2.9 in
1970 (Table 5). These results are attributable to the aging character of the

Table 3. Comparison of Wynnefield whites and blacks with respect to selected socio-economic and housing characteristics–1970 (tracts 117, 118 and 119 only).

Characteristic	Blacks	Whites
Median age	25.4	43.2
Average family size	3.7	2.6
Percentage of families with both husband and wife present	69.1	60.9
Percentage of female headed households	14.3	11.4
Median income*	$ 7,890	$ 8,665
Median educational level	11.9	12.0
Percentage of blue-collar workers	82.6	78.4
Percentage renting	12.7	14.8
Percentage in overcrowded dwellings	4.7	1.7
Percentage in multi-unit dwellings	20.4	55.3
Median property values*	$ 8,898	$ 9,926

* Median income and property levels reported in the census take into account the decreased purchasing power of the dollar in 1970 as compared to 1960.

Source: 1970 Federal census.

white population which was not completely counterbalanced by the in-migration of younger black families with children. These figures for the community as a whole mask important differences between Lower and Upper Wynnefield. In the Upper Hill section there was a decrease in family size, while in the Lower Hill section there was an increase (Table 5), reflecting the fact that racial change occurred more rapidly in Lower Wynnefield and that black families tended to be larger than white ones (Table 3).

A commonly expressed fear among whites in racially changing neighborhoods is that a disproportionately large number of the black arrivals will be female headed and on welfare, and that in general, racial change will be accompanied by an increase in family instability. These fears were not substantiated during the racial transition process in Wynnefield.

The census results (Table 5) do point to differences between white and black families with respect to family structure. A higher proportion of black than white families were single headed; but on the other hand, a higher proportion of black than white families had both husband and wife present. These results are confounded by differences between the black and white

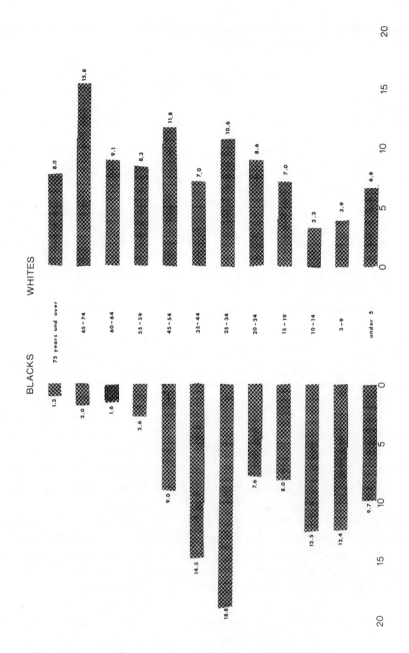

Figure 5. Black and white population by age.   *Source:* 1970 U.S. Census.

Table 4. Comparison of white and black Wynnefield families with respect to stage in life cycle.

Stage in life cycle	White	Black
Below 41 years, no children	11%	12%
Below 41 years, with children	13	44
41 years and above, with children	15	24
41 years and above, no children	61	20
	(148)	(50)

$x^2 = 31.4$
$df = 3$
$p < .001$

Table 5. Changes in the socio-economic characteristics of Wynnefield's population between 1960 and 1970.

Characteristic	Total community		Upper Wynnefield		Lower Wynnefield	
	1960	1970	1960	1970	1960	1970
Median age (years)	41.3	37.0	55.2	42.4	34.3	31.5
Average family size	3.0	2.9	2.9	2.5	3.0	3.2
Percentage of families with both husband and wife present	77.3	62.3	79.0	62.9	76.5	65.0
Percentage of children with both parents	82.6	77.3	86.5	87.0	92.4	74.5
Median income level	$7,523	$8,762	$9,638	$10,586	$6,598	$7,893
Median educational level (years)	11.2	12.1	11.9	12.4	10.8	11.9
Percentage of white collar workers	34.2	28.8	45.5	42.3	28.9	22.0
Percentage renting	29.6	37.2	39.9	54.3	24.9	27.6
Percentage enrolled in private or parochial schools	11.9	15.6	16.2	33.4	11.3	1.5
Percentage in overcrowded dwelling	1.1	2.8	0.7	1.3	1.3	3.7
Percentage in multi-unit dwellings	26.9	36.5	37.6	51.5	22.1	28.2
Median property values*	$13,118	$10,916	$19,316	$15,506	$10,864	$12,086

* 1970 median incomes and property values are adjusted to take into account the decreased purchasing power of the dollar.

Source: 1970 Federal census.

populations with respect to age structure (i.e., the fact that whites tended to be older). One would suspect that many of the single headed white families were elderly widows or widowers whose children had left home, while many of the black single headed households were young female headed families with children. Furthermore, this would imply that among young families with children, a higher proportion of black than white families would be single headed. If this were the case, it would substantiate the fears of whites. Table 6 does not, however support this line of reasoning, since there were no significant differences between blacks and whites with respect to family structure, holding family life cycle position constant. Young white families with children were as likely as blacks at that stage in the family life cycle to be single headed.

At first glance, Table 5 seems to support the fears of white residents that racial changes per se would lead to increased family instability. During the 1960's, there was a decrease in the proportion of families with both husband and wife present and a decrease in the proportion of children living with both parents. These results are inconclusive, however, because they can be explained in two different ways. These shifts might reflect the inmigration of some younger black female headed households with children. On the other hand, they might reflect the increasingly aging character of the white population. Since it is impossible to examine the census results in a more precise manner, it is impossible to determine which of the above two explanations is more valid.

2. Socio-economic characteristics

Previous studies of racially changing communities have emphasized the upwardly mobile character of black inmigrants and the degree of resemblance between them and long-term white residents with respect to socioeconomic characteristics. The census results support this earlier research. Although the median income level for blacks ($ 7,890) was somewhat lower than for whites ($ 8,665), the median educational level of adults was virtually identical (11.9 years for blacks and 12.0 years for whites).

One would suspect that the degree of similarity between whites and blacks with respect to these two socio-economic variables was attributable to differences in the age structures of the two populations. That is, the income and educational level of the white population might have been lowered due to the large proportion of elderly individuals or couples − combined with the fact that there is usually a negative correlation between age and both education and income. This suggests the possibility that if blacks and whites in the same age categories were compared, whites might typically have more formal education. Similarly, if whites and blacks at the same stages in the family life cycle were compared, whites might have higher income levels.

Educational differences do widen in the predicted manner when age is held constant. Among younger household heads (40 and below) a significantly higher proportion of whites (57 percent, 37) than blacks (26 percent, 27) had completed at least a B.A. degree (p<.03). (There were, however, no significant differences between whites and blacks in the 41 years and above category.) This finding for younger household heads reflects continuing differences in educational opportunities between blacks and whites.

Differences in family income also widen in the expected way when we take into account differences in family life cycle position. Table 7 shows that among families with household heads 41 years and older and with children, a significantly higher proportion of whites than blacks had incomes exceeding $ 10,000. These differences probably reflect the fact: (1) that whites tended to have more formal education; and (2) that whites were more likely to be in the better paying white collar jobs (as will be discussed shortly). This finding implies that middle age white families with children generally had more financial resources available for the home and children than was the case for comparable blacks.

White fears about racial change having an adverse impact on educational and income levels were not supported. Between 1960 and 1970, median family income increased by 16.5 percent (from $ 7,527 in 1960 to $ 8,762 in 1970), taking the decreased purchasing power of the dollar in 1970 into account.[7] Similarly, the average educational attainment increased from 11.2 years in 1960 to 12.1 years in 1970.

The most striking change in the socio-economic character of the population during the 1960's, was in the occupational composition of the population. During this period, there was a shift away from white collar occupations to blue collar work (Table 5). Table 3 shows that this shift was directly linked to the racial changes that occurred. As of 1970, a far higher proportion of black than white residents were in blue collar occupations (83 percent versus 78 percent). One would suspect that there were wider differences in occupational type among younger blacks and whites. As we have seen above, younger whites tended to have more formal education,

7. According to the Consumer Price Index, $ 100 in the base period 1957-59 was equivalent to $ 97.10 in 1960 and $ 74.00 in 1970.

Table 6. Comparison of white and black Wynnefield families with respect to family structure controlling for family type (proportions of families that are single-headed).

Family	White	Black	Sig. level
Below 41 years, no children	53% (15)	40% (5)	*
Below 41 years, with children	16% (19)	5% (22)	n.s.
41 years and above, with children	9% (23)	0% (12)	n.s.
41 years and above, no children	24% (89)	44% (9)	n.s.

* Too few cases to use the chi square test of statistical significance.

Table 7. Comparison of white and black Wynnefield families with respect to income controlling for family type (proportions of families with incomes of $10,000 or higher).

Family type	White	Black	Sig. level
Below 41 years, no children	47% (83)	83% (6)	*
Below 41 years, with children	53% (15)	60% (20)	n.s.
41 years and above, with children	85% (120)	50% (12)	.08
41 years and above, no children	37% (62)	25% (8)	n.s.

* Too few cases to use the chi square test of statistical significance.

and college degrees are often a prerequisite for better paying white collar jobs. Thus, younger white adults probably were more likely to have had white collar jobs than comparable blacks. Unfortunately, it was not possible to test for the validity of this line of reasoning because the telephone interview did not include detailed questions on occupational character-istics.

3. Housing characteristics
In the past, most black inmigrants to racially changing communities have become homeowners. This also occurred in Wynnefield. In 1970, the

proportion of blacks that owned (78 percent) was actually substantially higher than for whites (65 percent).

A priori, there would seem to be two explanations for the higher rate of homeownership among blacks. On the one hand, this finding might reflect the fact that a higher proportion of whites were in later stages of the family life cycle when it is fairly common to rent an apartment. If this explanation were valid, there would be insignificant differences in homeownership rates between blacks and whites at the same stage of the family life cycle. On the other hand, these differences in homeownership rates might be attributable to the fact that a disproportionately large number of the white inmigrants to the community (at all stages of the family life cycle) during the 1960's chose to rent, rather than own their home. This latter pattern has been observed in other racially changing communities (Rapkin and Grigsby, 1960: 54) and reflects the desire among whites to avoid the uncertainties of homeownership (including the possibility of experiencing a financial loss as a result of declining property values) in a racially changing area. If the second explanation were valid, then the homeownership rate for blacks would exceed that for whites even when family life cycle position is held constant.

Table 8 provides some support for the second explanation. Among younger families with children, a far higher proportion of blacks than whites owned. The fact that the results are not statistically significant is probably attributable to the small sample sizes in the specific life cycle categories.

There were even more pronounced differences between blacks and whites in housing type than there were with respect to tenant status. Whereas about one out of every five white families lived in an apartment

Table 8. Comparison of white and black Wynnefield families with respect to tenant status controlling for family type (proportions of families who are homeowners).

Family type	White	Black	Sig. level
Below 41 years, no children	19% (16)	67% (6)	*
Below 41 years, with children	68% (19)	86% (22)	n.s.
41 years and above, with children	91% (23)	92% (12)	n.s.
41 years and above, no children	74% (89)	90% (10)	n.s.

* Too few cases to use the chi square test of statistical significance.

(19 percent, 155) only about one out of fifty blacks lived in this type of building (p<.03). We would have liked to compare blacks and whites on housing type holding family life cycle position constant. It was not possible to do this, however, because there were so few black families living in apartments.

Given the higher rates of homeownership among blacks than whites, it is surprising that between 1960 and 1970 the rate of homeownership declined from 37 to 30 percent. This shift was attributable to the construction of apartments in the Upper Hill section of the community that proved attractive to white families without children.

3.3.2. The impact of racial change on community standards

The previous section has shown that in general, racial changes in Wynnefield did not adversely alter the socio-economic character of the population. These changes did, however, have a more marked negative impact on community institutions (e.g., the local public schools) and on community standards (e.g., the incidence of violent street crime).

1. The public schools

Previous case studies of racially changing communities have emphasized that racial change usually occurs more rapidly in the public schools than in the surrounding community. This is precisely what occurred in Wynnefield (Figure 6). Overbrook High School (located just outside the community) had a black majority as early as 1961, reflecting the fact that its attendance boundaries included much of predominantly black West Philadelphia (as well as Wynnefield). After 1957, it experienced a steady increase in the proportion of black students. By the early 1970's, the school was virtually all black. The junior high and two elementary schools in Wynnefield were predominantly white until 1965, when they experienced a sharp increase in the proportion of black students. By 1970, all three schools were predominantly black.

The fact that Wynnefield's schools underwent more rapid turnover than the community as a whole was attributable to two factors. Firstly, as mentioned above, Wynnefield's white population contained a disproportionately large number of middle aged and elderly couples (whose children presumably had left home). Secondly, during the 1960's, an increasingly large proportion of the white population adapted to racial changes by

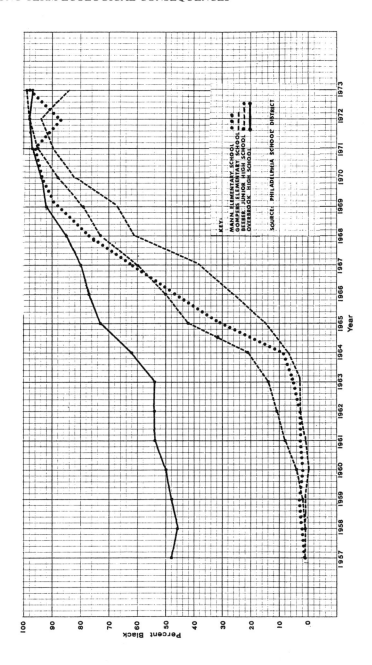

Figure 6. Changes in the racial composition of schools serving Wynnefield. (*Source*: Philadelphia School District.)

enrolling their children in private or parochial schools. In the predominantly white Upper Hill section, the proportion of children in private and parochial schools increased from 16 percent in 1960 to 33 percent in 1970.

The quality of Wynnefield's schools began to decline with the influx of large numbers of black students. Overcrowding and low test scores became two of the most serious problems facing the schools during the late 1960's and early 1970's. In all four schools serving Wynnefield, enrollment exceeded capacity (Table 9). In one of the elementary schools, Mann, the rate of overutilization was 134 percent in 1974. Because the Philadelphia Board of Education has only recently begun to administer standardized tests, it is not possible to measure changes in test scores. However, the results from the one test it has administered (the CAT test in 1974), suggest that the scores are low by middle class standards (Table 10). In only one school, Gompers Elementary, did more than one half of the students score above the 50th percentile. The scores were lowest in the junior and senior high school, which is not at all surprising since these schools draw students from poorer sections of the West Philadelphia ghetto (in addition to Wynnefield).

2. Housing conditions

Vacant homes became an increasing source of concern to residents during the late 1960's and early 1970's. (A vacant home is defined by the Office of Finance of Philadelphia as one that has been unoccupied for at least one year, regardless of its physical condition or marketability.)[8] Of the 116 vacant homes in the community in Spring, 1974, a large proportion were concentrated in the southern edge of census tract 119, but there were vacant homes in nearly every neighborhood (Figure 5). Many of the vacant homes were painted with graffiti which marred the appearance of the immediate neighborhood. Of more immediate concern to residents, is the

8. Personal communication, Office of Finance of Philadelphia, December 2, 1974. The Census Bureau also gathers information on housing vacancies. These figures are not used here because of their limited 'usefulness in analyzing neighborhoods having significant numbers of non-market vacant units. The Census Bureau eliminated from the total housing stock, those vacant units "..unfit for human habitation because the roof, walls, windows or doors no longer protected the interior from the elements or if there is positive evidence... the unit is to be demolished or condemned." Thus, the vacancy rate in neighborhoods with a large number of poor quality units is less than it would be had these units been included.' (Philadelphia City Planning Commission, undated: 25).

Table 9. Capacity and enrollment in Wynnefield schools 1974.

	Capacity	Enrollment	Over (+) or under (—) utilization
Mann	850	1139	134%
Gompers	650	768	118%
Beeber J. H. S.	1472	1700	115%
Overbrook H. S.	2900	3529	122%

Source: Philadelphia School District.

Table 10. CAT test scores for Wynnefield schools 1974.

	Test scores by percentile			
	85 or above	50-84	16-49	Below 16
Mann	10%	23%	42%	26%
Gompers	20	36	35	9
Beeber J. H. S.	3	15	44	38
Overbrook H. S.	2	17	36	45

Source: Philadelphia School District.

fact that they are often fire hazards and that they may be used by gangs in the area.

In addition, there was some increase during the 1960's in the degree of overcrowding (e.g., the proportion of families in dwellings having more than one person per room, see Table 5), and the rate of increase was particularly great in Lower Wynnefield. It is impossible to ascertain from the census data (on changes in household density), whether the overcrowding was severe enough to lead to a deterioration of the physical condition of the housing (see Taeuber and Taeuber, 1965: 164). Further, there is no evidence that overcrowding was accompanied by the subdivision of single-family homes into multiple-dwelling units (as has occurred in other transitional communities). While there was an increase during this time period in the proportion of housing in multi-unit structures in Upper Wynnefield (see Table 5), this generally reflected new apartment construction, rather than any significant degree of subdividing.

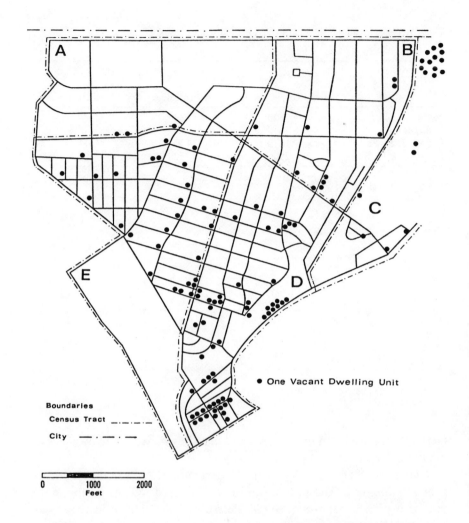

Figure 7. Vacant dwelling units

3. Property values

A frequently expressed concern of residents of racially changing communities is that racial change will lead to a decline in property values. There has been no single price reaction in racially changing areas. In some communities, prices have gone up following racial change, in other areas they have gone down. Wynnefield is one of those communities where racial change depressed property values. Between 1960 and 1970, the mean property value declined by 17 percent (from $ 13,118 to $ 10,916 taking into account the decreased purchasing power of the dollar in 1970).[9] In contrast, the average property value in Lower Merion Township during this period increased by 7 percent (from $ 25,945 to $ 27,753). The sellers of the large single-family homes in Wynnefield have had a particularly hard time finding purchasers (see Janson, 1973). Many have only been able to get back what they paid, sacrificing appreciation and the costs of improvements. Furthermore, many of these homes have sold for one half or one third of comparable homes in Lower Merion Township.

4. Street crime

Two recent studies of racially changing Jewish communities – Mattapan, Boston (Ginsberg, 1975) and South Shore, Chicago (Molotch, 1972) – have emphasized the impact of violent street crime on the community. Not surprisingly then, street crime has been the most important problem in Wynnefield during the 1960's and early 1970's. During the early 1960's, Wynnefield experienced a series of muggings and stabbings of elderly women. More recently, youth gang violence has claimed a number of lives. A survey conducted by the Jewish Federation of Philadelphia, *Jewish Exponent*, December 22, 1972) found that almost one third (31 percent) of a sample of elderly residents considered Wynnefield 'frightening.' Vandalism and other crime has forced many storeowners to close, and the local business district is now marred by many vacant storefronts.[10] Police statistics also provide an indication of the seriousness of the crime problem. Murder, rape, robbery and aggravated assault were far more common in

9. Our analysis of property values is limited to census information rather than actual market prices. Value as reported by the census, is the homeowner's estimate of how much his property, home and lot, would sell for, if put up for sale.
10. This conclusion is based on a survey of 54th Street businessmen completed Spring, 1971 by a graduate student in City Planning at the University of Pennsylvania.

Wynnefield than Lower Merion Township in 1973, despite the fact that Wynnefield's population was only about one third that of Lower Merion Township [11] (Tables 11 and 12). Furthermore, *total* crime (which includes

Table 11. Incidence of crime in Wynnefield, the 19th police district (which includes Wynnefield).

	% change 1960-65		% change 1965-73		Number of offenses (1973)
	19th District	Philadel-phia	19th District	Philadel-phia	Wynne-field
Homicide	+ 60%	+ 27%	+ 75%	+ 100%	5
Rape	+ 19	----	+ 56	+ 30	11
Robbery	+ 5	+ 39	—434	+ 193	107
Aggravated Assault & Battery	+ 47	+ 91	+ 56	+ 13	33
Burglary	—19	+ 40	+ 34	+ 53	245
Larceny	—11	+ 18	— 6	+ 8	199
Auto theft	+ 31	+ 126	+ 91	+ 117	254
Total	+ 31	+ 24	+ 91	+ 50	854

Source: Philadelphia Police Department.

Table 12. Incidence of crime in Lower Merion Township 1960, 1965, 1973.

	1960	1965	% change	1973	% change
Homicide	0	1	----	1	----
Rape	4	2	— 50%	1	— 50%
Robbery	6	13	+ 117	53	+ 308
Aggravated assault	7	8	+ 14	28	+ 250
Burglary	197	334	+ 70	617	+ 85
Auto theft	55	100	+ 82	191	+ 91
Total	744	1146	+ 35	1517	+ 32

Source: Lower Merion Township Police Department.

11. The boundaries of Wynnefield correspond fairly closely to those of four police sectors. Crime data, by sector, is unavailable prior to 1973. As a result, we utilize data on the 19th Police District (which includes these four sectors) in comparing changes in the incidence of crime between 1965 and 1973 for Wynnefield and Lower Merion Township.

other less serious crimes as well as those just mentioned) increased at a faster rate between 1965 and 1973 in the 19th Police District (encompassing Wynnefield and other sections of West Philadelphia, 57 percent) than in Lower Merion Township (32 percent).

3.4. Conclusions

One aim of this chapter has been to determine the degree of resemblance between the racial transition process in Wynnefield and the process in other middle-class communities that have been studied. In fact, the process has been fairly typical with respect to all three aspects of the process that have been investigated: (1) the factors that made Wynnefield susceptible to racial change; (2) the nature of stabilization efforts and their degree of effectiveness; and (3) the long term ecological consequences of racial succession. A second aim has been to identify the specifically Jewish aspects of the transition process. As we have seen, Wynnefield's ethnic composition has affected the community's susceptibility to racial change and has also influenced the way it has reacted to black inmigrants.

The key factor making Wynnefield susceptible for change was its proximity to an expanding black residential area – West Philadelphia. Given the sectoral expansion patterns of black residential areas throughout the United States it was inevitable that the community would undergo racial change as early as the 1950's. Wynnefield shared two other characteristics with other middle class areas that underwent transition during the 1960's and 1970's: (1) it contained a disproportionately large number of elderly residents; and (2) the row houses (which constituted the bulk of the housing in the community) were structurally sound but were viewed as obsolete by white residents.

Two Jewish cultural characteristics mentioned in previous research (Sklare, 1972; Caplan and Wolf, 1960) contributed to the area's susceptibility to racial change. Firstly, rapid socio-economic mobility enabled many Jewish families to move to higher status suburban areas. Secondly, there was a tendency among many Jews raised in Wynnefield not to live in the same community as their parents. This pattern conflicts with the widely accepted notion of the Jewish family as being strong and cohesive. (In contrast, it is fairly common for the children of Italian families to live in the same building or neighborhood as their parents.) It would have been interesting to examine as part of this chapter: (1) whether this pattern (not to live in the same neighborhood as the parents) is distinctively Jewish or whether it is typical of middle class American families generally; and (2) if the pattern is distinctively Jewish, the types of Jewish cultural variables that explain it. It was however, beyond the scope of this chapter to investigate these issues. Additional research dealing with these issues seems warranted.

Wynnefield's adaptation to black inmigration has been typical in two ways of other racially changing Jewish communities. Firstly, there has been no physical harassment of black arrivals – as has often occurred in other non-Jewish white ethnic communities. Secondly, the organized Jewish community in Philadelphia played a role – albeit a limited one – in stabilization efforts. Together, the Jewish Federation of Philadelphia and the Jewish Community Relations Council of Philadelphia allocated $ 4,000 to the Wynnefield Residents Association in the late 1960's and early 1970's. Interestingly, the Combined Jewish Philanthropies played a similar role with respect to the Mattapan Organization in Boston (Ginsberg, 1975). In addition, the Jewish Community Relations Council conducted an educational campaign aimed at reducing the fears of white residents and preventing them from panic moving.

As has been the case in racially changing Jewish communities throughout the United States, the stabilization efforts of Jewish agencies in Philadelphia have been largely ineffectual (see Sklare, 1971: 109). Between 1960 and 1970, the community changed from predominantly white to about one half white. Although racial change occurred more slowly in the Upper Hill section, this was largely due to the attractiveness of the homes rather than the efforts of the Residents Association or the Jewish Community Relations Council.

The goal of stable racial integration has not been achieved in Wynnefield for the same reasons it has not been achieved in other middle-class communities throughout the United States. The programs that have been implemented (usually through the Residents Association) have been inherently incapable of dealing with those metropolitan wide forces responsible for black housing demand being focused on the community: racial prejudice among suburban whites, and private and public institutional practices which have severely limited housing opportunities available to blacks in suburban areas.

As has usually been the case, racial change in Wynnefield has had a greater impact on community institutions and community standards than it has had on the socio-economic characteristics of the population. The public schools underwent rapid transition, property values depreciated, and there was a drastic increase in street crime. In addition, although no trend data is available, it appears that classroom overcrowding, low test scores and vacant housing became more serious problems during this period. In general, racial change did not adversely alter the socio-economic character of the population. During the 1960's, there were increases in income and educational levels.

The upward movement in income and educational levels during the 1960's was a reflection of the fact that the black and white populations *on the whole* resembled one another with respect to these two variables. These results – the similarity between blacks and whites with respect to income and education – are in line with previous research. They are deceptive, however, because they do not take into account differences in the age structures of the two populations. Wider differences emerged when blacks and whites of the same type were compared. Among younger household heads, whites had more formal education than blacks. Among middle age families with children, whites had considerably higher incomes.

The analysis revealed two other differences between the white and black populations. Firstly, whites were more likely to rent and live in apartments; while blacks were more likely to own and live in either attached or detached dwellings. Secondly, whites were more likely to be in white collar occupations, while blacks were more likely to be in blue collar work.

These findings emphasize the difficulty that policymakers will face in promoting stable integration in American central cities. It is assumed by many policymakers that stable racially mixed areas promote interracial social contacts. This chapter's findings from Wynnefield do not support this assumption. Even if the process of transition were stopped in Wynnefield (with its black-white ratio in 1970), it is likely that black-white social contacts would occur relatively infrequently. Neighborhood friendships are based upon common background characteristics and interests (e.g., in the family and home). The differences between blacks and whites in demographic characteristics and life style orientations, pointed out in this chapter, constitute important barriers to the development of meaningful social contacts between blacks and whites. The fact that many blacks and whites were spatially separated – due to the relatively large number of whites living in high rise apartments – means that many whites will lack even the everyday physical contact with blacks necessary as a first step toward the development of friendships.

The local resident association has been seen as one means by which social contacts between whites and blacks can be promoted. This chapter has indicated that a far higher proportion of blacks than whites are likely to become members of these organizations. Consequently, the resident association is likely to have only a limited influence in promoting black-white social contacts.

4. Determinants of moving plans: Did white residents panic move?

4.1. Introduction

The previous chapter described the speed and character of racial transition in Wynnefield. This and the following two chapters seek to explain these shifts. There is increasing consensus among researchers that in order to explain residential shifts of particular ethnic groups it is necessary to examine the mobility decisions of individual households. Consequently, this chapter focuses on three research questions related to the determinants of moving plans of white Wynnefield households:

1. To what extent was racial change associated with a tendency on the part of white families to accelerate their moving plans?
2. What family characteristics (including the family's religious identification) contributed to the willingness to remain?
3. To what extent did two Jewish religious characteristics – Jewish denominational affiliation and frequency of synagogue attendance – contribute to explaining variations in moving plans?

This chapter is based on the 1969 telephone survey of Jewish and non-Jewish residents of the Wynnefield-Lower Merion Township area. Since this chapter focuses on determinants of white moving plans; only the results from white respondents are utilized. The following section discusses the variables from the telephone interview schedule included in the analysis as well as the hypotheses tested.

4.2. Definitions of variables and hypothesized relationships

4.2.1. Dependent variable-moving plans

Household moving plans were measured by the question: 'How many years do you expect to remain at your current address?' The responses, given in number of years, were coded into nine categories ranging from less than three years to eighty or more. There was also a category for those who either did not know how long they would would remain or who refused to answer the question. In the analysis in this chapter the responses to this question were categorized into two groups: (1) those who planned to move within three years; and (2) those who planned to remain three years or more or who were uncertain about their moving plans.[1]

4.2.2. Independent variables

1. Family location

As part of the telephone interview schedule, the household was coded with respect to its location in one of the three study subareas (Wynnefield, southeastern Lower Merion Township, northwestern Lower Merion Township). In this chapter the household's location in one of these three areas is used to indicate the neighborhood racial context at this location. That is, a Wynnefield location is used to indicate a racially changing neighborhood, while a southeast or northwest Lower Merion Township location is used to indicate a stable predominantly white one. The attitudinal and objective data that are available (including census information) suggest that these were valid assumptions.

On the basis of previous research we assumed that the identification of a family as a Wynnefield resident would contribute to the likelihood of planning to move when all other personal characteristics were controlled.

2. Factors affecting the susceptibility of white mobility plans to racial change

a. Education

A common assumption made by planners and social scientists is that the

---

1. Several other approaches to recoding this variable were considered. The above version proved best in terms of two criteria: (1) maximizing the number of cases that could be utilized in the analysis (i.e., including those who were uncertain about their moving plans); and (2) yielding the highest possible beta coefficient between plans and behavior when other personal characteristics were included in the analysis. The crosstabular results indicated that those who were uncertain about their moving plans and those who planned to remain three years or more closely resembled one another in the likelihood of moving. Forty seven percent (53) of those who were uncertain about their moving plans moved as compared to forty percent (20) who planned to remain three years or more.

degree of racial prejudice[2] will influence a white household's decision of whether to remain in or move into a racially mixed community (Blumer, 1956:140; Sabagh *et al.*, 1969:92). Researchers have consistently found a negative association between formal educational attainment and the level of racial prejudice (Allport, 1958:223; Selznick and Steinberg, 1969:176, 179). Combining the assumption and the findings suggest that the level of formal educational attainment contributes positively to the family's willingness to remain in a mixed area.

b. *Presence of school age children*

Concern about decline in the quality of local public schools has been seen to be one of the most important factors affecting the moving plans of current and prospective white residents in middle class areas subject to racial change (Fauman, 1957; Wolf and Lebeaux, 1969). Parents with children already in the public schools would be expected to view such changes as more of a threat than those without children or with children in other age groups or in private school (Rose, mentioned in Rapkin and Grigsby, 1960: 36-37). Consequently, the presence of at least one school age child would likely be negatively associated with the willingness to remain in a racially mixed area.

c. *Housing type*

Studies of racially mixed areas have suggested that housing price and quality play a particularly important role in attracting and retaining white residents. White demand has been found particularly high where the housing offered better than average values for the money – and in particular, where comparable values were not available in suburban areas (Advisory Committee to the Department of Housing and Urban Development, 1972: 8; Guttentag, 1970; Rapkin and Grigsby, 1960; Bradburn *et al.*, 1971). This suggests that the types of housing available in Wynnefield would affect the willingness of whites to remain.

As noted in Chapter 1, Wynnefield is divided into two sections. The 'Lower Hill' section consists largely of attached homes but with some apartments. In the 'Upper Hill' section large and attractive detached homes predominate. At the time the original survey was conducted, the cost and value of the detached homes in the Upper Hill section seemed to make

---

2. Prejudice has been defined as an attitude of favor or disfavor and an overgeneralized belief about members of another group (Allport, 1958: 12-13).

them particularly attractive to middle and upper income whites. Based on the assumption (that these detached homes were perceived as values by resident whites) and previous findings, it was anticipated that the presence of a family in a detached home would be positively associated with a willingness to remain.

d. Religious affiliation

Researchers have noted that Jewish communities are particularly suscep-tible to black encroachment. Caplan and Wolf (1960) have suggested that Jewish communities undergo racial transition more rapidly than non-Jewish ones. This would imply that, among residents of a racially changing community, the identification of a family as Jewish would contribute to the likelihood of planning to move when all other factors were controlled.

e. Organizational participation

The social relationships between current white residents and their neighbors are likely to be affected by neighborhood racial changes. Fami-lies who emphasize participation in the neighborhood (a 'locality orienta-tion') probably would view racial changes as a more serious threat to their life style than those emphasizing social relationships throughout the city (a 'cosmopolitan orientation', Sabagh et al., 1969: 92). This would be so because racial changes might lead to sharp declines in membership of particular neighborhood organizations. Consequently, active neighbor-hood organizational participation would be expected to be negatively as-sociated with the willingness to remain in a mixed area.

In summary, five different family characteristics might affect the will-ingness of whites to remain in a mixed area: (1) formal educational level; (2) presence of school age children; (3) house type; (4) religious affiliation; and (5) neighborhood organizational participation. This chapter tests for the importance of these different characteristics.

3. Jewish religious characteristics affecting the susceptibility of moving plans to racial change

a. Jewish denominational affiliation

Respondents who identified themselves as Jewish were then asked for their Jewish denominational affiliation – Orthodox, Conservative, Reform or no particular denomination (i.e., 'just Jewish'). We assumed that the identification of the family as Orthodox would contribute to plans to remain. This hypothesis was based on case studies showing religious Jewish families as the last to move from racially changing communities (Johnson, 1974).

b. Synagogue attendance

The frequency of synagogue attendance was used as another indicator of the degree of religiosity of the family. That is, those families who attended synagogue fairly frequently were expected to be the more religiously observant ones. We expected a positive correlation between frequency of synagogue attendance and plans to remain.

4. Background characteristics affecting mobility generally

a. Life cycle position[3]

Researchers have generally found that for the metropolitan area as a whole, the most important determinant of voluntary moves is housing needs generated by life cycle changes (Simmons, 1968:636). 'For typical families, mobility propensity is highest during the family formation, child bearing and child launching phases (of the life cycle) and is least marked during the child rearing period – especially when the child is in school' (Sabagh, et al., 1969:92). In the past, researchers have frequently used age as an indicator for family life cycle position, and have found it to be negatively associated with mobility propensity (see for example, Roistacher, 1975). We also expected age to be negatively associated with mobility plans among Wynnefield residents.

b. Tenant status

Previous research has documented the higher mobility propensity of renters than owners (Pickvance, 1973: 287-288). Moore (1972) suggests

---

3. As part of the preliminary analysis, a new variable was computed to measure life cycle position from three separate characteristics: age of household head, presence of children under six, and presence of children six to seventeen. Using the results to these three questions, families were classified into four groups, those with: (1) heads 40 and under with no children at home; (2) heads 40 and under with children at home; (3) heads 41 and older with children at home; and (4) heads 41 and older with no children at home. We expected that family life cycle position (i.e., moving from positions 1 through 4) would be positively correlated with residential stability. This variable was not included in the regression equations in this chapter because it was far less powerful than age in predicting moving plans and because it was highly correlated with age. The bivariate crosstabular results for this and the other independent variables discussed in this chapter may be found in Appendix Table 3A.

that the lower mobility rate of owners is due to the economic, physical and psychological obstacles to moving. Our hypothesis was that homeownership would constitute a formidable barrier to moving among Wynnefield residents.

c. Duration of residence

We assumed that moving plans would be negatively correlated with the length of residence at the current location. In the past, researchers have found a negative correlation between duration of residence and moving propensity and attributed it to the fact that over time, the habits of families become established at one location, and they become increasingly reluctant to initiate a new pattern of living elsewhere (Moore, 1972; Sabagh *et al.*, 1969).

d. Family income

Adequate financial resources are an important prerequisite for moving (Sabagh *et al.*, 1969:94). Financial resources include, but are certainly not limited to, current family income. We expected family income to be negatively correlated with plans to remain.

e. Likelihood of job transfers

Most intermetropolitan moves are related to the employment situation of the family breadwinner (e.g., job transfers). As part of the survey, respondents were asked, 'Will you/your husband still work at the same place after your next move?' A 'no' response, was interpreted to mean that the head of the household expected to be transferred. We hypothesized that the expectation of a job transfer in the near future, would contribute to residential mobility.

4.3. Analysis

Stepwise multiple regression analysis is used in this chapter to explain variations in moving plans. This technique measures the contribution of each family characteristic, as well as the family's location in explaining moving plans – taking into account the interrelationships among these characteristics. The beta value (the standardized regression coefficient) indicates the strength and direction of the relationship between each independent variable and the dependent variables in the regression equation.

4.4. Findings

4.4.1. Moving plans and racial change

The crosstabular results suggest that there was a tendency on the part of white residents in Wynnefield to accelerate their moving plans in response to increases in the proportions of blacks in the surrounding area. While one tenth (10 percent) of the white families in Lower Merion Township planned to move within three years, about one third (30 percent) of the white families in Wynnefield planned to move during this period. The more rapid moving plans among white Wynnefield residents might conceivably have been due to differences in the population characteristics of the two areas. Renters, occupants of attached homes or apartments and families with young heads are shown to have relatively rapid moving plans (Appendix Table 3A). The differences in moving plans between the two areas may therefore have been attributable to the fact that Wynnefield contained a larger proportion of these three population subgroups.

The above explanation is not supported by the results of the regression analyses in Table 1. Personal characteristics alone account for 16 percent of the variance in moving plans for the study area as a whole. The age of the household head is the personal characteristic most strongly correlated with moving plans. When personal characteristics are considered along with family location the proportion of variance explained increases to 18 percent, an increase of 2 percentage points over and above the variance explained by just the personal characteristics. In addition, there is a significant beta coefficient between moving plans and location (Wynnefield or Lower Merion Township) when all other personal characteristics are controlled. Previously we mentioned the fact that the most striking difference between these two areas was the presence of racial change in Wynnefield and its absence in Lower Merion Township. The results therefore, strongly imply that white Wynnefield families were accelerating their moving plans in response to perceptions of increases in the proportion of blacks in their surrounding community.

4.4.2. Variables affecting the mobility plans of white families

1. Factors affecting the susceptibility of moving plans to racial change

As was anticipated, the educational level of the household head was an accurate predictor of moving plans among white Wynnefield residents.

Table 1. Results of regression analyses* relating moving plans (likelihood of remaining) with different personal characteristics and location for white respondents in the study area as a whole.

	Personal characteristics only				Personal characteristics and location			
	R square change	Unstandardized regression coefficient	Standard error of unstandardized regression coefficient	Standardized regression coefficient	R square change	Unstandardized regression coefficient	Standard error of unstandardized regression coefficient	Standardized regression coefficient
Age of household head	.0545	.0738	.0112	.3259**	.0545	.0723	.0110	.3196**
Housetype	.0600	.0980	.0345	.1384**	.0601	.0366	.0390	.0517
Location	—	—	—	—	.0188	.1688	.0445	.1905**
Tenant status	.0062	.1072	.0406	.1340**	.0168	.1436	.0414	.1795**
Likelihood of job transfer	.0087	.0509	.0203	.0965**	.0086	.0534	.0203	.1014**
Length of residence	.0082	-.0185	.0084	-.1043**	.0084	-.0187	.0083	-.1055**
Children six to seventeen	.0088	-.0550	.0310	-.0766**	.0028	-.0480	.0310	-.0668**
Jewish	.0069	.0269	.0702	.0379	.0021	.0141	.0704	.0198
Organizational participation	.0010	.0103	.0135	.0295	.0016	.0158	.0136	.0452
Children under six	.0008	-.0298	.0407	-.0324	.0011	-.0314	.0405	-.0342
Education	.0006	.0057	.0080	.0305	.0005	.0057	.0086	.0306
Protestant	.0006	.0057	.0080	.0305	.0001	.0470	.0690	.0662

Catholic	.0010	.0614	.0723	.0749	.0006	.0486	.0717	.0593
Income	***	***	***	***	.0006	−.0110	.0130	−.0419
Constant		.4437				.1931		
D.F.		614				614		
R²		.1568				.1765		
F Ratio		9.3415**				9.200**		

* The independent variables are highly inter-correlated. Appendix Table 3C presents the separate inter-correlations among these variables.

** F values significant at the .95 confidence level.

*** Variable was included in the computer run but not in the regression equation because the F level or the tolerance level was insufficient for further computation.

Definitions of variable in regression analysis: Moving Plans (0) plan to move within three years, (1) Plan to remain three years or more or uncertain about moving plans; Age of household head (categories reflect an increasing number of years); Location (0) Wynnefield, (1) Lower Merion Township; Likelihood of job transfer (0) Expect to be transferred, (1) Do not expect to be transferred; Tenant status (1) Rent, (2) Own; Children under six (1) One or more (2) None; Jewish — whether the family is Jewish (1) Yes, (0) No; Length of residence — duration of residence at current location (categories reflect an increasing number of years at the current location); Neighborhood organizational participation (1) Belong to none, (2) Belong to one or more; Children six to seventeen (1) One or more, (2) None; Housetype (1) Attached or apartment, (2) Detached; Family income (categories reflect increasing income levels); Protestant — whether the family is Protestant (0) No, (1) Yes; Catholic — whether the family is Catholic (1) No, (2) Yes; Educational level of household head (categories reflect increasing educational levels).

Table 2. Results of regression analyses* relating moving plans (likelihood of remaining) with different personal characteristics for white respondents in Wynnefield and Lower Merion Township.

	Wynnefield				Lower Merion Township			
	R square change	Unstandardized regression coefficient	Standard error of unstandardized regression coefficient	Standardized regression coefficient	R square change	Unstandardized regression coefficient	Standard error of unstandardized regression coefficient	Standardized regression coefficient
Age of household head	.1575	.1234	.0280	.4771**	.0446	.0546	.0120	.2635**
Likelihood of job transfer	.0241	.1979	.0841	.2134**	.0085	.0412	.0192	.0936**
Education	.0317	.0535	.0264	.2397**	.0003	−.0031	.0081	−.0178
Housetype	.0143	.1952	.1168	.1519**	.0010	−.0325	.0418	−.0480
Length of residence	.0120	−.0273	.0201	−.1294**	.0017	−.0090	.0087	−.0560
Organizational participation	.0098	.0585	.0410	.1259**	.0006	.0078	.0135	.0256
Catholic	.0108	.2742	.3155	.1826	***	***	***	***
Protestant	.0007	.1671	.3350	.0809	.0005	.0189	.0318	.0314
Jewish	.0010	−.1128	.2927	−.0937	.0020	.0237	.0351	.0349
Children under six	.0003	.0267	.1294	.0204	.0032	−.0434	.0401	.0547
Income	.0092	−.0469	.0431	−.1215	***	***	***	***
Children six to seventeen	***	***	***	***	.0050	−.0518	.0299	−.0839
Tenant status	***	***	***	***	.0599	.2008	.0450	.2817**

Constant	.2483	.2742
D.F.	110	500
R²	.2713	.1273
F Ratio	3.3846**	6.4967**

* The independent variables in these analyses are highly inter-correlated. Appendix Tables 3D and 3E present the separate inter-correlations between these variables for the Wynnefield and Lower Merion Township samples.

** F values significant at the .95 confidence level.

*** Variable was included in the computer run but not in the regression equation because the F level or the tolerance level was insufficient for further computation.

Table 2 shows that there was a significant positive correlation between educational level and plans to remain when all other personal characteristics were controlled. In the past, researchers have shown that racial prejudice is negatively correlated with educational level. If this were the case our finding (on the relationship between education and moving plans) would imply that racial prejudice was a key factor influencing the susceptibility of whites to racial change. There is however, another possible interpretation for this finding. It may reflect the fact that the more educated were concentrated in the Upper Hill section of the community and that residents of this area tended to be more optimistic about the area remaining racially mixed, rather than becoming predominantly black. Chapter 5 tests for the validity of these two interpretations by including in the regression runs, measures of racial prejudice, perceptions of the neighborhood's racial composition and expectations of racial and race related changes – in addition to the level of formal education of the household head.

As anticipated, the housetype of the family had a significant impact on mobility plans (Table 2). Families living in the detached single-family homes were far less likely to formulate plans to move than those living in attached homes or apartments. As we mentioned previously, the detached homes are highly attractive, on shaded streets and with large plots of land. Comparable homes cost up to twice as much in nearby suburban areas. On the other hand, the row homes in Lower Wynnefield appear shabby and probably were viewed as obsolete by most white residents. The results, therefore, suggest that a key factor holding whites to the area was the desire to maximize the quality of housing within available financial means.

In addition, the lower mobility propensity of detached home residents may have been due to the fact that they were more optimistic about their section of the community (the Upper Hill area) remaining racially mixed, rather than becoming predominantly black. Although the market for detached single family homes was depressed as a result of racial change, the cost of the homes was still beyond the purchasing power of most home seeking black families from West Philadelphia. Thus, it would have been realistic for whites to anticipate that the detached home area would continue to attract middle-class whites and relatively few blacks.

The presence of at least one school age child was not shown to contribute to the family's intentions of moving from Wynnefield. Earlier in this chapter it was hypothesized that the presence of school age children decreases the willingness of white families to remain in mixed areas. This suggests that there would be a positive relationship between the lack of any school age children and intentions to remain in Wynnefield. In fact, there was such a weak correlation between this variable and moving plans that it was not included in the regression equation.

There are two possible explanations why neighborhood racial changes did not have a disproportionately greater impact on families with school age children. One is that a large proportion of the white families did not send their children to local public schools. Some may have sent their children to private or parochial schools which draw their students from a relatively wide area, and as a result, were not as strongly affected by neighborhood racial changes.[4] Others may have kept their children in the Philadelphia school system, but either sent them to a predominantly white school in a nearby area or to one of Philadelphia's two 'elite' academic high schools (which were and still are predominantly white). Parents who sent their children to these Philadelphia public schools probably did not feel threatened by changes in the racial composition of local public schools.

Another possible explanation is that parents with school age children may have been reluctant to move because such a move would require transferring the child to another school system. These parents may have been fearful of the problems of adjustment involved.

The limited data gathered as part of the telephone interviews did not allow for a test of the validity of the above alternative explanations.

There is no evidence to support the hypothesis that the identification of a family as Jewish contributed toward an increased propensity to move from Wynnefield. Table 2 shows that there is a very weak negative correlation between the identification of the family as not Jewish and plans to remain among Wynnefield residents – whereas a strong correlation had been anticipated. This table also shows that – as anticipated – there was a fairly strong (but not statistically significant) beta coefficient between the identification of the family as Catholic and plans to remain. This finding might reflect the fact that many of the Catholic families sent their children to parochial schools and therefore were not seriously affected by racial changes.

Contrary to what had been expected, active neighborhood participation did not contribute to plans to move. In fact, Table 2 shows that those who belonged to one or more community based organizations were the least likely to move. This latter finding is in line with research on the deter-

4. Chapter 3 provides some support for this assertion. In the predominantly white Upper Hill section the proportion of children attending private or parochial school doubled between 1960 and 1970 (from 16 to 33 percent).

minants of mobility in stable middle-class communities. In this type of residential environment, active neighborhood social participation has been shown to constitute an important barrier to moving (Moore, 1972; Sabagh *et al.*, 1969).

2. Factors affecting mobility generally

As anticipated the age of household head had a significant impact on mobility plans (Table 2). In fact, age was the most important variable in the regression equation as indicated by the size of the beta coefficient and the R square change. Older household heads were far less likely to formulate moving plans than younger ones. The residential stability of older families probably reflects the fact that they were more reluctant to disrupt the patterns of life that they had established at their current location.

Table 2 supports the hypothesized importance of expectations of job transfers in influencing mobility plans. Household heads who anticipated a job transfer within the near future were far more likely to plan to move than those who did not expect to be transferred. This finding suggests that at least some of the moves among white Wynnefield residents were economically motivated.

The results provide no support however for the two other general mobility factors included in the analysis. Length of residence at the current location was negatively correlated with the likelihood of planning to remain, rather than positively correlated as had been anticipated. Among Wynnefield residents, tenant status had no bearing at all on the formulation of moving plans. Owners and renters were equally likely to plan to move. It is interesting to contrast this result with the one for Lower Merion Township where tenant status was one of the most important predictors of behavior. These findings taken together suggest that while homeownership may constitute a barrier to the formulation of moving plans in a stable white middle class community, it does not constitute such a barrier in a racially changing area like Wynnefield. The surprisingly strong tendency of renters to remain probably reflects the fact that many of the renters lived in the new high rise apartments in the community where they were isolated, to a certain degree, from racial changes in the surrounding community. Furthermore, these families did not have to face the prospect of experiencing declines in property values. As we saw in Chapter 3, this was a real problem for homeowners in the community during the 1960's.

4.4.3. Jewish religious characteristics affecting the susceptibility to racial change

Contrary to what had been expected, neither of the two indicators of the degree of Jewish religiosity – whether the family identified itself as Orthodox and the frequency of synagogue attendance – had a significant influence on moving plans (Table 3). The correlations between both of these variables and moving plans were so small that they were not included in the regression equations.

These insignificant results may reflect the fact that these two variables were inaccurate indicators of the level of religiosity of the family. It is likely that many of the families identifying themselves as Orthodox were only nominally Orthodox.[5] That is, they may have only identified themselves in this way because they belonged to an Orthodox congregation. In other respects – adherence to traditional Jewish beliefs and practices – they may not have differed significantly from other Jewish families. Similarly, there are a number of reasons for attending synagogue – religious convictions, as a basis for ethnic identification, and for social purposes. This suggests that the frequency of synagogue attendance may have been only an imprecise guide to the level of religiosity of the family. In order to more directly test for the impact of Jewish cultural and religious characteristics on mobility, Chapter 5 includes three attitudinal and behavioral measures in the regression analysis: the degree of observance of Jewish traditional practices, the attitude toward intermarriage and the attitude toward driving to the synagogue on the Sabbath.

4.5. Conclusions

This chapter has sought to determine whether an increase in the proportion of blacks in Wynnefield led current white residents to accelerate their moving plans. Secondly, it has sought to identify those family characteristics that promoted a willingness on the part of whites (Jews and gentiles) to remain in Wynnefield. Thirdly, it has sought to determine the importance of

---

5. Marcus (1967:13) states that many Jews 'join synagogues for social, educational and "folkist" reasons, if not out of a sense of piety... Membership in any one of them (Orthodox, Conservative, or Reform), if not a matter of chance, is a matter of familial attachment, and the demands upon the members in terms of religious practice are no greater in one synagogue than another.'

Table 3. Results of regression analyses relating moving plans (likelihood of remaining) with personal characteristics (including Jewish cultural characteristics) for Jewish Wynnefield respondents.

	R square change	Unstandardized regression coefficient	Standard error of unstandardized regression coefficient	Standardized regression coefficient
Age of household head	.1156	.1388	.0402	.4714**
Length of residence	.0281	—.0417	.0304	—.1939
Likelihood of job transfer	.0299	.1830	.1228	.1711**
Neighborhood organizational participation	.0249	.0704	.0514	.1536
Housetype	.0225	.1750	.1423	.1429
Education level of household head	.0151	.0379	.0308	.1685
Non-denominational Jew	.0167	—.1399	.1156	—.1489
Children under six	.0035	—.0921	.1960	—.0592
Children six to seventeen	.0018	—.0409	.1512	—.0357
Reform Jew	.0012	—.0523	.1754	—.0360
Tenant status	.0003	.0224	.1449	.0221
Income	***	***	***	***
Orthodox Jew	***	***	***	***
Conservative Jew	***	***	***	***
Synagogue attendance	***	***	***	***
Constant		.2302		
D.F.		71		
R²		.2595		
F Ratio		1.9437**		

* The independent variables in this analysis are highly inter-correlated. Appendix Table 3G presents the separate inter-correlations among these variables.
** F values significant at the .95 confidence level.
*** Variable was included in the computer run but not in the regression equation because the tolerance level or the F level was insufficient for further computation.
Definitions of variables in regression analysis: Non-denominational Jew — whether the family identifies itself with no particular Jewish denomination (0) No, (1) Yes; Orthodox Jew — whether the family identifies itself as Orthodox (0) No, (1) Yes; Conservative Jew — whether the family identifies itself as Conservative (0) No, (1) Yes; Reform Jew — whether the family identifies itself as Reform (0) No, (1) Yes; Synagogue Attendance (1) Less than seven times a year, (2) Once in one or two months, (3) More than once a month.
See Table 1 for definitions for the remainder of the variables in the analysis.

Jewish denominational affiliation and the frequency of synagogue attendance in explaining variations in moving plans among Jewish residents. Multiple regression analysis was utilized to examine the determinants of moving plans. Three principal conclusions may be drawn from this chapter.

1. There was a strong correlation between the location of the family in the study area and moving plans. Residents of Wynnefield had more rapid moving plans than comparable families in Lower Merion Township. This result strongly suggests that white residents of Wynnefield had accelerated their moving plans in response to racial changes. Consequently, racial turnover was occurring in this community as a result of both a decline in white demand for housing in the area and a speedup in white outmigration.

2. Two family characteristics – the educational level of the household head, and housetype (i.e., whether the family lived in a detached home) – significantly contributed to intentions to remain. Two other characteristics were also hypothesized to contribute to plans to remain – the lack of any school age children and relatively low levels of community participation. The analysis provided no evidence to support these hypotheses.

3. Jewish denominational affiliation (i.e., the fact that the family identified itself as Orthodox) and frequency of synagogue attendance did not have a significant impact on the likelihood of remaining. These insignificant results probably reflect the fact that these two variables are imprecise measures of the level of Jewish religiosity. Consequently, these findings do not necessarily mean that Jewish cultural and religious characteristics have no bearing on the likelihood of remaining in a racially mixed area.

5. The determinants of mobility: Do ethnic variables influence the decision to move?

5.1. Introduction

Recently, an advisory panel to the United States Department of Housing and Urban Development indicated that relatively little was known about the importance of different race related attitudes (including but not limited to racial prejudice) in affecting the willingness to move into racially mixed communities (National Academy of Sciences, 1972). This statement is equally valid concerning the state of existing knowledge about the influence of these factors on the willingness to remain in racially changing communities. Three race related attitudes have been mentioned in the literature as affecting the willingness to remain: (1) racial prejudice; (2) perceptions of the neighborhood's current racial composition; and (3) expectations of future racial changes. Few, if any, studies however have examined the relative importance of these characteristics in explaining variations in mobility in particular racially changing communities. This will be one of the major aims of this chapter.

The second purpose of this chapter is to examine the impact of the 'ethnic factor' in affecting mobility decisions in racially changing Jewish communities. In a widely quoted article, Simmons (1968: 633) notes: 'The ethnic factor acts as a constraint only on the number of possible alternatives, explaining "where" people move rather than "why" they move.' In fact, there have been few empirical tests of Simmons' assertion. This chapter examines the importance of two Jewish cultural characteristics – (1) the attitude toward intermarriage; and (2) the attitude toward driving to the synagogue on the Sabbath – in explaining variations in mobility among Jewish Wynnefield residents. Previous researchers have speculated that these two factors are crucial in affecting the choices of Jews as to where to move. We will test whether they also influence the decision of when to move from this racially changing community. The results dealing with these two Jewish cultural characteristics should be suggestive as to whether background cultural characteristics influence the move-stay decision in other (non-Jewish) white ethnic communities undergoing racial change.

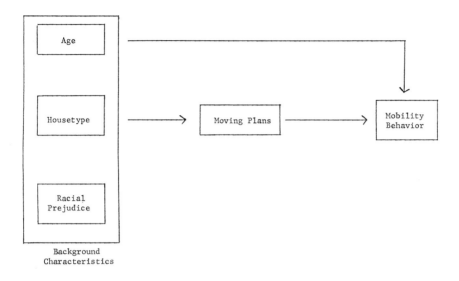

Figure 1. Mobility model.

This chapter also has a methodological purpose. Most previous mobility studies have relied on the relationships between background characteristics and moving plans (or moving desires). There is increasing consensus among researchers that these two variables (i.e., moving plans and moving behavior) are distinctive, and that research relying on plans as a proxy for behavior may provide a limited understanding of the mobility process (Van Arsdol *et al.*, 1968). Our approach is to view moving desires, plans and behavior as a set of interrelated decisions (Butler *et al.*, 1964). Utilizing this conceptual framework, this chapter seeks to determine which background characteristics affect mobility indirectly (through their impact on moving plans which are then implemented) and which affect mobility directly (i.e., affect the decision to move without having any effect on moving plans, Figure 1). In a previous article, we utilized this approach to examine the determinants of mobility in an inner city community (Varady: 1975). This chapter utilizes this same approach to examine the underlying causes of mobility in a racially changing community.

5.2. Methodology

This chapter is based on data from the 269 Jewish families who completed the 1969 mailed questionnaire and who participated in the 1974 follow-up effort. Since our focus is on the causes of mobility in racially changing communities, the analysis is limited to the results from Wynnefield residents only.

The analysis utilizes mobility related characteristics from the 1969 mailed questionnaire *as well as* the 1969 telephone interview schedule. Since Chapter 4 discussed the mobility characteristics from the telephone interview schedule, the following section is limited to characteristics drawn from the mailed questionnaire.

5.3. Definitions of variables and hypothesized relationships

5.3.1. Dependent variables

1. *Mobility behavior.* As part of the 1974 mailed questionnaire, respondents were asked whether they had moved from their 1969 locations. Even where no questionnaire was returned, it was often possible to ascertain the family's mobility behavior between 1969 and 1974 using telephone directories, forwarding information provided by the post office and synagogue membership lists. Altogether, using these different methods, it was possible to obtain mobility information on 81 percent (or 217) of the original 269 families who participated in the 1969 survey. Using these different methods from the 1974 follow-up effort, respondents were classified into two groups: (1) moved; and (2) did not move.

2. *Moving Plans.*[1] On the basis of previous research, we anticipated that there would be a fairly close correspondence between moving plans and behavior (Rossi, 1955; Van Arsdol *et al.*, 1968; Varady, 1974) and that plans to stay would be more accurate as predictors than plans to move.

5.3.2. Independent variables

A. *Factors affecting the susceptibility of white moving decisions to racial change*

1. *Racial prejudice.* Based on Bogardus' social distance scales (1925,

1. Chapter 4 discusses the way in which this variable was measured and coded.

1928, 1953) this study developed two scales to measure racial preju-dice.[2] The first scale measures the attitudes of householders toward living in a racially mixed area under differing assumptions about the income levels of black families. The second measures the attitudes of householders toward sending their children to racially mixed schools under differing assumptions about the test scores of the black children.

On the basis of previous research, we anticipated that these two measures of racial prejudice would not be accurate predictors of behavior. In other words, we did not expect those with 'liberal' attitudes toward racial resi-dential integration (i.e., who were interested in the idea when black families had incomes at least equal to theirs) to be less likely to move than those who held negative views on this subject.

2. The specific questions used to measure attitudes toward housing and educational integration were as follows:

How would you feel about living in a community where about 20% of the families were black (and the percentage was not increasing)? Would you be very interested, somewhat interested, somewhat against, or very much against the idea?

Circle one of the numbers after each statement

	Very interested	Somewhat interested	Somewhat against	Very against
If most of the black families had incomes below that of your family	4	3	2	1
If most of the black families had incomes about the same as your family	4	3	2	1
If most of the black families had incomes greater than that of your family	4	3	2	1

How would you feel about sending your child (assuming that you had one) to a school where 20% of the school children were black (and the percentage was not increasing)? Would you be very interested, somewhat interested, somewhat against, or very against the idea?

Circle one of the numbers after each statement

	Very interested	Somewhat interested	Somewhat against	Very against
If most of the black children had test scores below that of your child	4	3	2	1
If most of the black children had test scores about equal to that of your child	4	3	2	1
If most of the black children had test scores above that of your child	4	3	2	1

(Continued on following page.)

2. *Current neighborhood racial composition.* As part of the mailed questionnaire, respondents were asked to estimate the approximate racial composition of their immediate neighborhood. The five precoded response categories ranged from 'none but our family' to 'almost all of the families'. We anticipated that the proportion of whites in the immediate vicinity would be correlated with residential stability.

3. *Future racial changes.* Mailed questionnaire respondents were asked

These two scales represent an attempt to respond to two criticisms of scales used to measure racial prejudice in previous studies. Firstly, most of the scales that have been used have contained statements dealing with a number of different attitudes (racial stereotypes, attitudes toward discrimination, sympathy with the plight of blacks, (see Selznick and Steinberg, 1969: 170-175). Westie (1952), has noted that racial prejudice is a composite of several components. This implies that the validity and sensitivity of the scales will be increased if the scales measure subcomponents of prejudice (rather than attempt to use only one scale to measure racial prejudice). He identified four separate social distance scales to measure racial prejudice: Residential Distance, Interpersonal-Physical Distance, and Interpersonal-Social Distance. Furthermore, he suggested that an individual's social distance from blacks may vary depending on the socio-economic characteristics of blacks. Thus, it is important for the researcher to look at different occupational and racial combinations (e.g., a black doctor, a black laborer) in determining the relative importance of each component in assigning social distance. The two separate scales that have been used in this study to measure racial prejudice, incorporate features of Westie's social distance scales. The first – the attitude toward residential integration – measures the Residential Distance component of prejudice. The second – the attitude toward educational integration provides one possible indicator of the Interpersonal-Social Distance component of prejudice. Parents have relatively little control over whom their children will choose as friends at school. The willingness to send children to an integrated school may, therefore, be used as a measure of the willingness of a parent to permit social interaction between their children and black children. In addition, following Westie's suggestion, our scales include different income, social class and racial combinations. That is, respondents were asked about their attitudes toward residential integration under differing assumptions about the income levels of the black families, and their attitudes toward educational integration, under differing assumptions about the test scores of the black children. (We assumed that differences in the test scores of the black children reflect differences in the black childrens' social class background.)

Secondly, most questions which have been used to measure the willingness to live in a hypothetical racially mixed community have not specified the racial composition of the area. We assumed that the willingness of a respondent to live in a racially mixed community is dependent upon the racial composition of that community and the rate of turnover from white to black. Similarly, we expected that the interest of whites in school integration would be dependent on the racial composition and rate of turnover of the student body. In order to insure that the respondents interpreted the questions similarly, the questions specified the community racial characteristics. Respondents were asked to assume that the community/ school was 20% black and the proportion was not increasing. The stable 20 percent figure was used in both cases because we felt it to be beyond the level of token integration, but below the point where whites might move away simply because of the proportions per se.

The results for the tests of Guttman scalability for these and other Guttman scales in this chapter are to be found in Appendix Table 4A.

whether they thought the proportion of blacks in the immediate vicinity of their home would increase, remain the same or decrease in the next five years or so. We assumed that the expectation of an increase in the proportion of blacks would be correlated with residential mobility.

The questionnaire included several other items dealing with race related changes. The following beliefs were assumed likely to contribute to residential mobility, that the:
- proportion of Jews would decrease
- typical income would be lower in five years, and
- property values would decline.

4. *Income contextual position.* Reference group theory may be utilized to explain migration decisions in neighborhoods experiencing social and economic changes. This would include, but not be limited to, racially changing communities. Reference groups are 'those groups to which the individual refers himself as part or to which he aspires to relate himself psychologically' (Sherif and Sherif, 1953:161). It is assumed that one's neighbors may provide the basis for self-evaluation. The individual is assumed to implicitly estimate his deviance from others with respect to some characteristics of the group. Where the neighborhood is the significant reference group, and where there is a perception of too large a discrepency in some salient characteristics between residents in the surrounding area and the household (possibly because of the characteristics of the new inmigrant families), the household would be expected to be more inclined to move than if no such discrepency existed.

Up to this point, research on the impact of the income contextual position of families on moving decisions has been inconclusive. Øyen, (1964) studying four residential areas of Oslo, Norway, found no significant association between either the income or occupational contextual position of the household and its attachment to the area. We assumed, nonetheless, that the income contextual position of Wynnefield whites might influence their mobility propensity. The income contextual position of the family was computed by subtracting family income from the perceived typical neighborhood income level. (Both questions, family income and perceived neighborhood income had the same five precoded categories, ranging from under $5,000 to $25,000 or more.) We anticipated that to the extent that family income deviated from the typical family income level (either upward or downward) this would contribute to residential mobility.

5. *Satisfaction with shopping facilities.* Chapter 3 indicated that in Wynnefield (as in other racially changing communities), transition has been accompanied by a deterioration in the quality of shopping in the local commercial district. Kosher butcher shops and other stores serving a Jewish clientele have closed, symbolizing the disappearance of the Jewish community.

The mailed questionnaire respondents were asked about their level of satisfaction (ranging from very satisfied to very dissatisfied) with three aspects of neighborhood shopping: (1) the time required to get to the stores; (2) the types of goods and services; and (3) the comfort of shopping. A scale was developed to measure the overall level of satisfaction with neighborhood shopping by summing the number of items marked 'very satisfied'. We assumed that the level of satisfaction with neighborhood shopping facilities would contribute to residential stability.

6. *Neighborhood participation.* In Chapter 4, we hypothesized that families pursuing a locality oriented life style were more likely to move than those pursuing a cosmopolitan life style. The mailed questionnaire included two indicators of a locality oriented life style: (1) the number of relatives in the immediate vicinity; and (2) the number of friends in the immediate vicinity. We assumed that both measures would be correlated with residential mobility.

B. Jewish religious and cultural characteristics affecting the susceptibility of mobility decisions to racial change

1. *Attitude toward intermarriage.* The attitude toward religious endogamy (marrying within the group) is likely to be a good indicator of the extent to which the household head desires to separate his family from the broader community and be part of the Jewish subcommunity. If the head segregates his family in this way, its friends would be largely limited to other Jewish families in the area. Social ties to these other families are likely to constitute an important reason for remaining.

Religious changes accompanying the turnover of a Jewish community are likely to increase the possibility that Jewish children will meet, date and possibly marry gentiles. This threat is likely to be least serious among religious families (i.e., those with a strict attitude toward intermarriage) because under normal circumstances, that is, in a stable predominantly white area, they are likely to exert fairly strong controls over their children's selection of friends.

A Guttman scale measuring this attitude was computed from the results to five separate items on the survey. Respondents were asked whether they would approve of a male friend of theirs marrying a gentile in five situations, ranging from where the prospective wife was going to convert to Judaism to where the male friend was going to convert to Christianity. We expected that a strict attitude toward intermarriage (i.e., a low score on this scale) would contribute to residential stability.

2. *Attitude toward driving to the synagogue on the Sabbath.* Under traditional Jewish law, it is forbidden to drive on the Sabbath. Orthodox interpretation forbids driving on the Sabbath, whereas it is permitted in Conservative or Reform Judaism. The need to be within walking distance of a congregation is, therefore, an important basis for residential clustering among the Orthodox. We would expect that a strict attitude toward driving on the Sabbath would contribute to residential stability in racially changing communities. These families would not have the option of moving from the community and then driving back for religious services.

The mailed questionnaire included a set of three items (forming a Guttman scale) dealing with the attitude toward driving to the synagogue on the Sabbath. Respondents were asked whether they would approve or disapprove of someone driving to the synagogue where: (1) the individual lived within a short walk of the synagogue; (2) where he would find it inconvenient (but not impossible) to walk; and (3) where he lived beyond walking distance from a synagogue. We assumed that a positive score on this scale (i.e., a tolerant attitude toward driving) would contribute to residential mobility.

3. *Observance of Jewish customs.* Previous research suggests that the least assimilated – and hence, the most religious Jewish families – would be least likely to move from a racially changing community. The mailed questionnaire contained a series of five items (forming a Guttman scale) dealing with the degree of observance of these practices: (1) having a *sedar* in the home; (2) lighting *Hanukah* candles; (3) lighting Friday night Sabbath candles; (4) having a *mezuzah* on at least one door of the house; and (5) buying meats only from a kosher butcher. Our hypothesis was that a positive score (i.e., a fairly high level of observance) would be correlated with residential stability.

C. Background characteristics affecting mobility generally[3]

1. *Accessibility to work.* Planners and economists usually have assumed that accessibility to work influences residential choices. This would imply that the desire to be closer to the job would influence moving decisions within the same commuting area (Brown, 1975; Roistacher, 1975). As part of the mailed questionnaire, respondents were asked about the extent to which they were satisfied with three different aspects of commuting – the time, expense, and comfort involved. A scale was developed to measure the overall satisfaction with commuting by summing the number of items marked very satisfied. A second measure of satisfaction with accessibility was computed by subtracting the amount of time the respondent said he spent commuting from the maximum time that he said he would be willing to spend commuting. (Both questions had the same eight precoded response categories ranging from one to nine minutes to seventy minutes or more.) We assumed that to the extent that the time spent commuting exceeded the maximum specified, this would contribute to residential mobility.

5.4. Analysis

In order to explain variations in mobility behavior among Wynnefield residents, regressions were run using moving plans, then moving behavior as the dependent variables and the background characteristics discussed in the previous section as the independent variables.[4] We first ran the regressions with all the background characteristics discussed in the previous sections as the independent variables. These results are presented in Table 1. We then reran the regressions, excluding those variables that did not meaningfully contribute to explaining variations in behavior.[5] These latter

3. As mentioned earlier, the analysis also included those general mobility factors measured on the telephone interview schedule.

4. The crosstabular results are presented in Appendix Table 4B.

5. In general, we excluded those variables whose F values were statistically insignificant at the .05 level. There were two exceptions to this generalization. Firstly, we included householders' perceptions of their neighborhood's racial composition in later runs even though the F values were not statistically significant. We did this because of the theoretical importance of this variable combined with the fact that the beta value between this variable and moving plans was quite large.

  Secondly, we excluded the number of relatives in the immediate vicinity even though the F

regression results are represented by a path diagram (Figure 2).[6] The hypothesized causal relationships are represented by unidirectional arrows extending from each determining variable to each variable depending on it. Residual variables are represented by vertical unidirectional arrows from the residual variable to the dependent variable. Standarized regression coefficients are placed alongside the unidirectional arrows (with an indication of whether the coefficients are statistically significant). Since the coefficients are standarized, the two paths leading to the same variable can be compared by order of magnitude to indicate which variable has the most powerful direct effect. The non-causal factors in the system are represented by two headed curvilinear arrows.

5.5. Findings

5.5.1. Factors affecting the susceptibility to racial change

As expected, the two indicators of racial prejudice were not accurate predictors of behavior. Table 1 shows that there were negligible correlations between both moving plans and mobility behavior on the one hand and attitudes toward housing and educational integration on the other.

value was statistically significant for the relationship with mobility behavior. We did this because the results dealing with moving plans were in the opposite direction. With such contradictory results, it was felt proper to exclude this variable from later regression runs.

We were conscious of the fact that we might encounter multicollinearity by including so many background characteristics in the regression analysis. In reality, this was not a serious issue in our analysis. Firstly, extreme multicollinearity did not exist (i.e., intercorrelations between .8 and 1.0). Secondly, where there was moderate multicollinearity (i.e., intercorrelations between .5 and .6) we used one variable as a proxy for others. Specifically, the initial regression run (see Table 1) indicated that there was moderate multicollinearity between perceptions of the neighborhood's current racial composition and expectations of racial, religious and income changes, as well as possible changes in property values. It also showed that perceptions of the neighborhood's current racial composition was far more powerful in explaining variations in mobility plans and mobility behavior than the other four variables. Consequently in the next regression run – the one used to prepare the path diagram (Figure 2) – perceptions of the neighborhood's racial composition served as a proxy for the other four.

We were also aware of a second methodological issue. That is, that regression analysis assumes that all relationships are linear and additive whereas some of these relationships may conceivably be nonlinear and multiplicative. On the basis of the mobility model used in this volume it seemed reasonable to assume that the relationships would not depart from the linearity assumption. Therefore, we did not modify any of the variables, using for example, log transformations.

6. This discussion of path diagrams is drawn from Land (1969).

Table 1. Simple associations and relative importance of background characteristics in predicting moving plans (likelihood of remaining 3 yrs. or more) and mobility (likelihood of remaining between 1969 and 1974) for Jews in Wynnefield.

	Moving plans		Mobility behavior		
	Correlation	Beta	Correlation	Beta excluding moving plans	Beta including moving plans
Age	.05	.38**	.12	.22	.13
Children under 6 (whether have none)	.00	—.09	.12	.07	.09
Children 6 to 17 (whether have none)	—.08	***	.03	.05	—.05
Housetype (whether live in detached home)	.26*	.17	.23**	.20	.16
Tenant status (whether own)	.07	.09	—.05	—.07	—.09
Family income	.18*	—.02	.07	***	***
Education	.03	***	—.01	.11	.10
Length of residence	.00	—.14	—.02	—.07	.10
Organizational participation (whether none)	—.07	***	—.08	***	***
Number of relatives in vicinity	—.22*	—.10	.09	.21	.23**
Number of friends in vicinity	.15	—.07	.13	.15	.16
Likelihood of job transfer (whether don't expect transfer)	.03	.13	.01	—.10	—.14
Degree of interest in housing integration	—.02	.02	.05	.22	.21
Degree of interest in educational integration	—.13	.06	—.06	—.22	—.23
Proportion of whites in vicinity	.12	.32	.23*	.12	.04
Likelihood that the proportion of blacks will decrease	.00	.07	.12	—.02	—.03
Likelihood that the proportion of Jews in vicinity will increase	.00	—.29	.17*	.17	.24
Likelihood that property values will increase	.03	.22	.11	.03	***
Likelihood that typical income will increase	.10	—.08	.02	—.12	—.10
Income contextual position (likelihood that family income is lower than neighborhood)	.06	***	.09	.17	.16
Degree of tolerance of intermarriage	—.17*	—.30**	.06	.14	.21
Degree of tolerance of driving to the synagogue on the Sabbath	—.09	—.09	.13*	.09	.11

	Moving plans		Mobility behavior		
	Correlation	Beta	Correlation	Beta excluding moving plans	Beta including moving plans
Time to work vs. preferences (likelihood that the trip to work is less than the time specified)	.07	.21	—.18*	—.27*	—.32
Degree of satisfaction with commuting	.11	.10	.04	—.03	—.06
Degree of satisfaction with neighborhood shopping	.06	—.07	.15	.03	.04
Moving plans (to remain three years or more)	----	----	.19*	----	.24**
Constant		.38		—.07	—.21
DF		56		56	56
R²		.24		.35	.40
F Ratio		.55		.89	.96

* Kendall's correlation coefficient statistically significant at the .05 level.
** F values statistically significant at the .05 level.
*** Variables not included in the regression equation because the F level or the tolerance level was insufficient for further computation.

Respondents who were interested in living in a racially integrated neighborhood or in sending their children to a racially integrated school were just as likely to move as those who held negative views on these subjects. These results clearly support previous research showing that racial prejudice is a relatively unimportant factor in influencing mobility choices.

These findings can be better understood if one recalls how racial prejudice was measured in our study. Respondents were asked about their level of interest in living in a hypothetical stably integrated community with a white majority. This type of hypothetical situation did not correspond to that actually experienced by many of the Wynnefield respondents (particularly those in the Lower Hill section, where rapid racial change had occurred during the 1960's). These residents perceived their neighborhoods as changing and many lived in neighborhoods that were predominantly black. Thus, the insignificant results partly reflect the sharp disparity between the type of community preferred by those with pro-integration sentiments, and the type of community in which they were situated.

These results also may be interpreted in terms of previous research showing no necessary relationship between prejudice and discriminatory behavior (Berelson and Steiner, 1964: 505). (Withdrawal from a racially

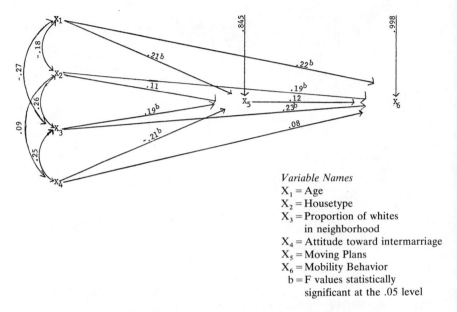

Variable Names
X_1 = Age
X_2 = Housetype
X_3 = Proportion of whites
       in neighborhood
X_4 = Attitude toward intermarriage
X_5 = Moving Plans
X_6 = Mobility Behavior
b = F values statistically
    significant at the .05 level

Figure 2. Path analysis of the effects of background characteristics and moving plans on residential mobility (likelihood of remaining) among Wynnefield residents.

mixed area can be considered a form of discrimination.) Prejudiced individuals may have decided to remain in Wynnefield and ignore black neighbors or discriminate against them by, for example, excluding them from participation in the local residents association or by both.

The findings support the hypothesized importance of perceptions of the neighborhood's current racial composition in influencing the move-stay decision. Figure 2 shows that this variable (X_3) had both a strong indirect and direct impact on mobility. That is, respondents who perceived that they lived in neighborhoods that were at least one half black, were far more likely to develop and implement plans to move than those living in neighborhoods that still had white majorities. In addition, some of the respondents who lived in substantially integrated neigborhoods made rapid decisions to move even though they had planned to remain. The respondents in substantially integrated neighborhoods who moved, probably did so because they were unwilling to be part of a racial minority. They may have also feared that if they remained, they would be part of a *tiny* racial minority in the future.

Contrary to what had been anticipated, expectations of racial and race-related changes did not significantly contribute to explaining variations in mobility behavior in the analysis (Table 1). There were insignificant beta coefficients between both moving plans and moving behavior on the one hand and expectations of (1) future racial changes; (2) future changes in neighborhood income levels; (3) future changes in the neigborhood's religious composition; and (4) future changes in property values.

The fact that this set of factors did not play a significant explanatory role may have been due to the fact that the study took place six years after the racial transition process had begun in Wynnefield. Thus, by 1969, the prospect of complete neighborhood racial turnover was a reality to residents rather than a distant possibility. Had these questions (dealing with expectations) been asked earlier in the transition process, they may have been shown to be more important in explaining variations in mobility.

Contrary to what had been anticipated, the income contextual position of the family did not have a significant impact on the likelihood of moving (Table 1). That is, those whose incomes deviated downward or upward from the typical neighborhood income level were not more likely to move than those whose incomes corresponded to the norm.

There is also no evidence that dissatisfaction with neighborhood shopping, resulting from the deterioration of Wynnefield's commercial district, contributed to many mobility decisions. There were insignificant beta coefficients between both moving plans and moving behavior and the overall level of satisfaction with neighborhood shopping facilities.

The results dealing with neighborhood participation variables are contradictory and inconclusive. Table 1 shows that, contrary to what had been expected, families with a large number of relatives in the immediate area were significantly less likely to make rapid decisions to move. This implies that the presence of these relatives nearby held families to the area. However, Table 1 also shows that families with relatives nearby were more likely to have planned to move. There is no obvious explanation for these contradictory results. The two other measures of neighborhood participation – the number of friends in the vicinity and the number of organizations to which members of the family belonged – played insignificant roles in explaining variations in mobility behavior.

As anticipated, the housetype of the family (X_2) had a significant direct impact on mobility (Figure 2). Families living in the detached single-family homes were far less likely to make rapid decisions to move. This result is similar to one presented in Chapter 4 related to determinants of moving plans. It reflects the fact that the homes in the Upper Hill section constituted unusual housing values and the fact that residents of that section were more optimistic about their neighborhoods remaining integrated, rather than undergoing complete racial turnover.

There is no evidence to support the hypothesized importance of another background characteristic – the presence of school age children – in influencing residential mobility. There were negligible beta coefficients between this variable and the two mobility measures and it, therefore, was not included in the regression analysis.

Earlier, we had hypothesized that individuals with a strict attitude toward intermarriage would be the ones most likely to move from a racially changing community. Table 1 and Figure 2 show, however, that a strict attitude toward this subject, indirectly contributed to decisions to remain. That is, individuals with a strict attitude toward intermarriage were significantly more likely to develop and implement plans to remain. This somewhat surprising finding can be explained in terms of previous research showing religious families to be the last to move from racially changing communities. The lower mobility rate of religious families reflects the fact that they usually have a greater sense of allegiance to their synagogue and stronger social ties to their Jewish neighbors. The low mobility rate of religious families in Wynnefield probably reflects another factor; that even if they wanted to move, there were (and are) only a few communities in the Philadelphia area that they could relocate to and remain within walking distance of a congregation.[7]

There was no evidence that the attitude toward driving to the synagogue on the Sabbath had any bearing on the likelihood of moving. Those who had a strict attitude (i.e., who were unwilling to approve of it under any conditions) were as likely to move as those who had a lenient attitude toward the subject.

5.5.2. Factors affecting residential mobility generally

As anticipated, the age of the household head (X_1) had significant, indirect and direct impacts on mobility (Figure 2). Older household heads were far less likely to develop and implement moving plans than younger ones. They were also less likely to make rapid decisions to move. The residential stability of older families probably reflects the fact that they were more

7. Religious families in a racially changing Jewish community in Detroit faced an analogous situation (Wolf, 1965). Theirs was the last remaining identifiably Jewish community in the city.

reluctant to disrupt the patterns of life that they had established at their current locations.

None of the other general mobility characteristics measured on the telephone interview schedule (i.e., tenant status, length of residence at the current location, family income, and likelihood of a job transfer) significantly contributed to explaining variations in mobility behavior (Table 1). Similarly, the two measures of accessibility to the job (measured on the mailed questionnaire) were of no explanatory importance. The results for the variable 'time to work versus preferences' were just the opposite of what had been anticipated. Household heads who spent less time commuting than their stated maximum were more likely to move rather than less likely as had been assumed. These latter results imply that few of the respondents moved to be closer to their jobs. Although these findings do contradict our hypothesis (as well as the results of two recent studies (Brown, 1975; Roistacher, 1975) these results are actually in conformance with most research on the subject (Moore, 1972).

5.5.3. Moving plans

The relatively large beta coefficient between moving plans and moving behavior (Table 1) indicates that plans independently contributed to explaining variations in behavior when all other background characteristics are taken into account.[8] Furthermore, moving plans account for explaining an additional 5 percent of the variance in mobility beyond that explained by background characteristics alone. The fact that moving plans independently contributed to explaining variations in behavior, probably reflects

8. The F ratio for moving plans is not statistically significant in Figure 2 even though it is in Table 1. This seeming discrepency is due to the fact that in Table 1 the impact of moving plans includes the joint influence with other variables. When the list of background characteristics is reduced (as is the case between Table 1 and Figure 2) it is not surprising that the impact of moving plans decreases.

The bivariate crosstabular results dealing with the relationship between moving plans and moving behavior are of interest. Seventy-one percent of those who planned to move in less than three years (N=14) had moved by 1974, whereas only 40 percent of those who planned to remain three years or more (or who were uncertain about their moving plans, N=73) had moved. The rate of correspondence between moving plans and behavior in this study, 58 percent, is lower than for previous research on the subject (i.e., where it has been found to be between 70 and 80 percent). Contrary to what had been expected, plans to move were more reliable predictors than plans to stay. Some of the respondents who planned to remain for the foreseeable future may have decided to move when it became apparent that racial change was occurring more rapidly than they had anticipated.

the fact that moving plans were affected by a variety of personality characteristics not measured on the survey (e.g., chronic restlessness). Had more of these characteristics been measured and included in the regression analysis, the independent impact of plans on behavior would have been considerably reduced.

5.6. Summary

This chapter has sought to add to the existing limited knowledge on the relative importance of different racial and ethnic attitudes and other background characteristics in explaining mobility behavior in racially changing communities. It has also attempted to determine the way in which these characteristics influence behavior. That is, which factors affect mobility indirectly through their impact on plans (which are then implemented) and which factors affect mobility directly. Multiple regression analysis was utilized to determine the relative importance of different race related attitudes, Jewish cultural characteristics and other background characteristics in explaining variations in mobility behavior among Jewish residents of the Wynnefield section of Philadelphia.

Four major conclusions emerge from the analysis:

1. One of the most important determinants of mobility behavior was the householder's perceptions of the neighborhood's current racial composition. Whites that lived in neighborhoods that were 50 percent or more black were far more likely to move than those in neighborhoods with fewer blacks. This finding parallels previous research showing few whites willing to move into or remain in substantially integrated communities.

2. The level of racial prejudice was not an accurate predictor of mobility behavior. Those interested in residential and educational integration were just as likely to move as those who held negative views on these subjects. These results, therefore, provide additional evidence (to that in earlier research) that there is a sharp difference between one's attitude toward integration in general, and one's attitude toward living in a particular racially changing community. The reason for this discrepancy has to do with what the respondents (and most white Americans) consider a desirable integrated community – that is, one that has a stable white majority. Many of the Wynnefield respondents would have been willing – if not eager – to remain if their community remained integrated with a white majority. Since many of the neighborhoods in Wynnefield (particularly in the Lower Hill

section) were at least one half black by 1969, the pro-integration senti-ments of white residents were largely irrelevent.

3. The family's housetype had a great bearing on the likelihood of remaining. Households living in the large attractive detached homes in Upper Wynnefield were far less likely to move than those living in the attached homes or apartments. Detached home residents probably re-mained because comparable housing in nearby suburban areas would have cost considerably more. Previous research has shown that the desire to obtain the best apartment or house within one's means is a key factor in the choice of where to move (Bradburn, *et al.*, 1971). It appears that this factor is also important in deciding whether to move from a mixed community.

4. Finally, a strict attitude toward intermarriage contributed to decisions to remain. This finding supports previous research documenting the resi-dential stability of religious Jewish families in racially mixed neighbor-hoods. The greater residential stability of religious families in Wynnefield probably reflects (a) the strong sense of allegiance to their synagogues and their strong social bonds to other religious families in the vicinity; and (b) the limited number of communities to which they might move (i.e., the fact that they could only consider areas where they would be within walking distance of a synagogue).

This latter finding appears to refute Simmons' assertion that ethnic variables affect only the decision of where to move and not the decision of when to move. It implies that cultural and religious characteristics may affect the mobility decisions of other types of white ethnic Americans besides Jews. Clearly, future research needs to be directed at explaining variations in the determinants of mobility in different types of racially changing white ethnic communities – as well as the underlying similarities involved.

6. The mobility process:
Why householders think they moved

6.1. Introduction

This chapter represents an extension of our analysis of the causes and characteristics of the racial transition process in middle class communities. In previous chapters, we have examined the determinants of mobility among white residents in this type of community; that is, the relative importance of different demographic, housing and attitudinal characteristics (e.g., racial prejudice) in explaining variations in moving plans and actual mobility behavior. This chapter examines residential mobility from another perspective: the reasons for moving provided by the residents themselves. We focus on three stages of the mobility process: (1) the decision to move from the former residence; (2) the search for a new home; and (3) the actual choice of where to move.

This approach to the study of mobility – i.e., where the focus is on reasons provided by the subjects – has been termed 'reason analysis'. This is a set of procedures used by survey researchers to study the causal relationships involved in an action based on perceived motives supplied by respondents (Kadushin, 1968). In this type of analysis, the action or decision is broken into phases, based on an underlying theory or model. Respondents are queried about the factors affecting each phase. In his classic mobility study published in 1955, Rossi utilized reason analysis to study household moves, but his study did not include any racially changing neighborhoods. Since that time, there have been few applications of this technique to transitional communities (for an exception to this generalization see Thomas and Simon, 1976). This chapter is directed at this gap in existing research.

6.2. Methodology

This chapter is based largely based on the sample of 154 families completing both the 1969 and 1974 surveys. Since the focus is on the mobility process, the analysis is based on the results from the 42 families (27 percent of the total) who moved during this period. More specifically, the analysis focuses on a section of the 1974 survey dealing with the three stages of the mobility process mentioned above.

Respondents were first asked whether they had, in fact, moved from their 1969 locations. Those who had moved were asked about their complaints with their 1969 location that had led to the move. They were provided with a list of 22 housing and neighborhood related characteristics which (on the basis of previous research) would be expected to affect the migration decision. They were asked to indicate whether these characteristics were very important, somewhat important or not important at all in this migration decision. Respondents were presented with a similar list to identify criteria used in the housing search. Subsequent questions dealt with: (1) information sources used in the housing search; (2) types and numbers of areas considered; (3) time spent in the housing search; and (4) the location of the family home chosen.

One part of this chapter (Table 5) is based on a larger sample of families who completed the 1969 mailed questionnaire and for whom mobility information was available. This includes the families who moved and who completed the 1974 survey plus those whose mobility behavior was ascertained using other sources: telephone directories, forwarding information provided by the post office, and synagogue membership lists. Altogether, using these different methods, it was possible to obtain mobility information on 81 percent (or 217) of the original 269 families who participated in the 1969 survey.

6.3. Hypotheses

6.3.1. Distinctive aspects of the mobility process in a racially changing community

1. *White panic moving.* It has been widely assumed by both social scientists and laymen that the racial transition process involves white panic moving. That is, once the proportion of blacks exceeds a certain point – the 'tipping point' – the white outmigration rate accelerates. We, therefore, anticipated that Wynnefield and Lower Merion movers would differ in terms of their complaints about their previous locations. Lower Merion residents would be more likely to mention 'normal' types of complaints related to the home itself (e.g., not enough space). On the other hand, Wynnefield residents would be more likely to mention the existence of racial change or problems

related to it (e.g., declines in the quality of local schools).

2. *Importance of different race related reasons for moving.* A number of researchers have studied the types of beliefs and concerns that whites develop about the surrounding residential area when the proportion of blacks increases. The beliefs and concerns mentioned in the literature include the expectation: (1) that property values will decline; (2) that the area will eventually become all or nearly all black; (3) that income levels and the status level of the area will decline; (4) that the quality of education at the local public schools will decline; and (5) that the area will experience physical deterioration. Recent case studies suggest that the most serious concern is about violent street crime. In her study of the racially changing Mattapan section of Boston, Ginsberg (1975) found that street crime had made life unbearable for the remaining white residents, and that the fear of street crime was based on reality. We, therefore, assumed that physical safety would be the most frequently mentioned complaint among Wynnefield movers.

3. *Criteria utilized in the housing search.* Previous studies have indicated that 'the criteria specified by the household (for the housing search) reflect the motivations of the decision to seek a new residence' (Moore, 1972:3). This would imply that there would be strong relationships between the stated reasons for moving from the 1969 location and the criteria used in the housing search. More specifically, this would mean that Wynnefield residents who moved because of the existence of racial change in the surrounding area would be particularly concerned about the racial composition of prospective locations. On the other hand, Lower Merion residents who moved because of complaints about the home would be particularly concerned about housing characteristics at new locations.

4. *The evaluation of alternatives.* Time is an important element in the search process. Among forced movers, 'the sheer necessity of providing a roof over their heads imposes a substantial time constraint' (Moore, 1972:18). It would seem reasonable to assume that the situation of families moving from a racially changing community would be somewhat analogous to forced movers. That is, if the quality of life deteriorates rapidly (for example, if a member of the family is assaulted or the house robbed), they may feel the pressure to purchase or rent the first dwelling they see that meets their standards. This implies that Wynnefield movers would have

spent less time in their housing search and would have seriously considered fewer locations than Lower Merion movers.

5. *Geographical scope of the housing search.* Previous research indicates that families usually concentrate their housing search in nearby areas, and secondarily, in the same sector of the city (Moore, 1972). We expected the same pattern in the study area although we anticipated that relatively few respondents would look for homes in Wynnefield because of the existence of racial change in that area.

6.3.2. Jewish ethnic characteristics and the mobility process

As we mentioned in an earlier chapter, it is widely believed that ethnic variables influence where people move not why or when they move. This would suggest that Jewish cultural characteristics would affect the types of areas considered in the housing search as well as the area finally chosen, but would not affect the decision to move. That is, the more religious families would probably confine their housing search to areas of relatively high Jewish density in the northern section of Wynnefield (near the city boundary) or to immediately adjoining areas in Lower Merion Township. They would do this to insure that there would be a sufficient number of Jewish families in the immediate vicinity to insure that their social life could be largely confined to other Jewish families.

In the last chapter, we found that one Jewish cultural characteristic, the attitude toward intermarriage, was important in explaining variations in mobility among Wynnefield residents. This suggests that this variable (or some other Jewish religious/cultural characteristic) would be associated with the types of reasons provided for moving from a Wynnefield location. More specifically, we would assume that the more religious or identifiably Jewish families would be more likely to cite as reasons for moving such factors as declines in the number of Jewish families in the area and the closing of synagogues in the area.

6.4. Findings

6.4.1. The decision to move

Table 1 provides support for the hypothesis that Wynnefield whites would

Table 1. Home and neighborhood related reasons for moving from the 1969 location.

	Wynnefield		Lower Merion Township	
	Prop. mentioning as very impt. (N = 14)	Rank	Prop. mentioning as very impt. (N = 9)	Rank
Crime	88%	1	78%	1
Racial change	62	2	25	13
Neighborhood reputation	60	3	67	5
Accessibility-ease of commuting	58	4	33	11
Shopping facilities	56	5	22	14
Quality of public schools	54	6	0*	17
Amount of space (too much or too little)	53	7	56	7
Cost of maintenance	46	8	56	8
Religious change (decline in the proportion of Jews)	46	9	0*	19
Cost of buying (and financing)	43	10	76	4
Neighborhood appearance	40	11	67	6
Layout of the dwelling	36	12	78	2
Exterior appearance of home	33	12	56	9
Quality of construction	29	13	67	3
Relatives—declines in the immediate area	29	14	0	21
Class composition—most of the residents of a different income or educational level	23	15	11	15
Property values— expected to decline	23	16	38	10
Friends—declines in the immediate area	23	17	0	20
Quality of private schools	15	18	0	18
Synagogues—declines in membership, closing of facilities	15	19	11	16
Age composition—most of the residents of a different age	8	20	0	19
Neighbors not friendly	0	21	25	12

* Chi square statistically significant at the 95 percent confidence level.

move in response to racial change, rather than simply for normal mobility reasons. This table compares Wynnefield and Lower Merion Township movers in terms of the proportions considering each of the housing and neighborhood factors as very important. This table also indicates the ranking of each of these factors, broken down by location, based on the proportions mentioning the factors as very important. As shown, a far higher proportion of Wynnefield than Lower Merion residents mentioned the following neighborhood related characteristics as very important in their decisions to move: that the community was undergoing racial change, that the quality of public schools and neighborhood shopping facilities were declining and that the community was experiencing declines in the proportion of Jewish families. These findings generally parallel the results from Chapters 3 and 4 where we found: (1) that Wynnefield respondents had more rapid moving plans than comparable families in Lower Merion Township; (2) that an important factor affecting the moving decision was the perception of the neighborhood's current racial composition; and (3) that racial change was accompanied by declines in the quality of local public schools and by a deterioration in the quality of the local business district. Whereas Wynnefield residents were more likely to move as a result of racial and race related changes, Lower Merion Township residents were more likely to move as a result of dissatisfaction with the quality of their home. This is shown by the fact that a far higher proportion of Lower Merion Township than Wynnefield residents mentioned the following three aspects of housing quality as very important to their mobility decision: the lay-out of the dwelling, the quality of the construction and the exterior appearance of the home.

The fear of crime was the most important reason for moving among both Wynnefield and Lower Merion Township respondents. Ninety percent of the Wynnefield respondents and eighty percent of the Lower Merion Township respondents considered this factor to be very important in their migration decision. The fact that safety was mentioned so frequently among Wynnefield respondents is as anticipated. As was shown in Chapter 3, there was, in fact, a sharp increase in the incidence of violent crime in Wynnefield in the late 1960's and early 1970's. The results for Lower Merion Township are surprising in that the actual incidence of violent street crime in this area was quite low in the 1960's and 1970's. This surprising finding might reflect the increasing concern of suburbanites throughout the nation about the crime problem, (see Delaney, 1976). On the other hand, it might reflect the fact that Wynnefield's crime problem actually spilled over into adjoining areas of Lower Merion Township, or that the residents believed that it would spill over into this area. If this latter explanation were valid, one would expect that most of the Lower Merion Township respondents who mentioned crime as a reason for moving would have lived in one of the Lower Merion Township communities adjoining Wynnefield. This is, in fact, what occurred. Of the eight Lower Merion Township residents who mentioned crime, seven lived in communities immediately adjoining Wynnefield. With the data at hand, it is impossible to determine whether these householders mentioned crime because they believed the incidence had increased in their area, or because they believed that it would increase in the near future.

It is important to stress that Wynnefield families did not move solely because of racial change (and related impacts on the community). They frequently moved for this reason combined with the need for less space. Space problems were a relatively important reason for moving among both Wynnefield and Lower Merion Township residents. Slightly over one half of the movers in both areas mentioned this factor (Table 1). It is not uncommon for older families to move to smaller quarters when their children leave home. Given the aging character of the Jewish population in the Wynnefield area, one would suspect that families who moved for space usually moved because they had too much space. This expectation is supported by the results to a set of four questions on the survey. Householders were asked whether any of the following family related reasons were responsible for their move: (1) widowhood; (2) more children at home; (3) fewer children at home; and (4) the retirement of the breadwinner. Table 2 shows that a far higher proportion of both Wynnefield and Lower Merion Township respondents mentioned the fact that there were fewer, rather than more, children at home. This same table indicates that more Lower Merion Township than Wynnefield moves resulted from the retirement of the breadwinner. Thus, it appears that many of the older Jewish families in Wynnefield would have moved away even if racial changes had not occurred. The fact that the community was undergoing ethnic change and (most importantly), that the security problem was worsening, probably hastened these decisions.

Earlier, we hypothesized that Jewish cultural characteristics influence the reasons for moving from a racially changing community like Wynnefield (e.g., that a decline in the number of Jewish families would be particularly important to religious families). This expectation was supported; the attitude toward intermarriage, between Jews and gentiles, was the most im-

Table 2. Family related reasons for moving from the 1969 location.

Reason	Proportion mentioning reason as important	
	Wynnefield (N = 16)	Lower Merion Township (N = 9)
Widowhood	8%	0%
More children at home	8	0
Fewer children at home	67	56
Breadwinner retired	17	44

portant explanatory variable. Respondents with a strict attitude toward intermarriage more frequently mentioned religious changes as a reason for moving than those with a lenient attitude (43 percent, 14 versus 12 percent, 17). Parents with strict attitudes probably were concerned about religious changes because they would increase the possibility that their children would meet and date gentiles. Secondly, these householders were probably the ones emphasizing a social life confined to other Jewish families. These families may have been concerned that as a result of declines in the number of Jewish families in the area, it would become more difficult to maintain an adequate social life.[1]

6.4.2. The search for a new home

1. *The criteria for evaluation.* We assumed that the criteria used in the housing search would be a function of the reasons for moving from the original location. If this hypothesis were valid, a far lower proportion of Wynnefield movers would have been concerned about the characteristics of the home itself in choosing new locations. Table 3 supports these expectations by comparing the proportions of Wynnefield and Lower Merion residents mentioning the different neighborhood and housing factors as very important. A far higher proportion of Wynnefield residents mentioned the racial and religious composition of the neighborhood and the quality of

1. In Chapter 5, we showed that a strict attitude toward intermarriage contributed to decisions to remain. It might appear at first glance that the finding conflicts with the one presented here (i.e., that those with a strict attitude were more likely to mention religious changes). In fact, no real discrepency exists since the analysis in this chapter is limited to families who moved. It appears that, in general, this attitude promoted residential stability, but that among the relatively few householders with a strict attitude who moved, religious changes in the area were a serious matter of concern.

Table 3. Housing and neighborhood related reasons for choosing the new location.

	Wynnefield		Lower Merion Township	
	Prop. mentioning as very impt. (N = 20)	Rank	Prop. mentioning as very impt. (N = 10)	Rank
Safety from crime	91%	1	80%	1
Religious composition	71	2	22	17
Convenience to work/ease of commuting	68	3	40	12
Neighborhood appearance	65	4	40	11
Shopping facilities	62	5	50	9
Neighborhood reputation	60	6	50	8
Layout of dwelling	58	7	73	3
Racial composition	57	8	22	16
Amount of space in dwelling	50	9	73	2
Cost of maintenance	50	10	50	7
Quality of public schools	50	11	20	19
Cost of buying (and financing and/or renting the dwelling)	47	12	64	5
Exterior appearance	45	13	40	10
Quality of construction	42	14	60	6
Property values	42	15	60	4
Class composition	33	16	10	21
Relatives (relatively large number in immediate area)	29	17	10	22
Synagogues (convenience of the location to a congregation)	26	18	30	15
Quality of private and parochial schools	17	19	10	20
Age composition	20	20	20	19
Neighbors friendly	15	21	30	13
Friends (relatively large number in immediate area)	11	22	30	14

the local public schools as very important in choosing their new location. A higher proportion of Lower Merion Township residents mentioned the amount of space in the dwelling, the lay-out of the dwelling, the costs of owning or renting the dwelling and the quality of construction as very important criteria in the housing search. Both Wynnefield and Lower Merion Township respondents were highly concerned about safety from street crime in their search for a new location. Nine tenths of Wynnefield respondents and eight tenths of the Lower Merion Township respondents considered this factor to be very important.

This hypothesis is also supported by the fact that there were strong relationships between the stated reasons for moving from the 1969 location and the criteria used in the housing search. Families that moved because of space problems were more likely to consider this factor as important in the housing search than those who did not move because of space problems (94 percent, 18 versus 20 percent, 15). Similarly, those who moved because of racial changes were far more likely to seriously consider this factor in exploring new locations than were those who did not move for this reason (79 percent, 15 versus 6 percent, 16).

A comparison of Tables 1 and 3 indicates that religious variables were more important in selecting a new location than in deciding to move from the original location. Less than one half (46 percent) of the Wynnefield residents mentioned religious changes as very important in their decision to move. In contrast, seven tenths (71 percent) mentioned the religious composition of the area as a very important factor in choosing their new location. These findings probably reflect the fact that in deciding whether to move, families were primarily concerned about racial change per se rather than other changes in the social composition of the population that were accompanying racial change (e.g., changes in the religious composition of the population). In choosing new locations, householders were concerned with finding stable white areas, but this left many areas as possibilities. The search was narrowed by insisting that the area have a sufficient number of Jewish families (this number varied) so that the family (including the children) could have Jewish friends in the area.

Table 3 shows, however, that few of the respondents were concerned about the accessibility to synagogues at new locations. Only about one fourth of the Wynnefield respondents and one third of the Lower Merion Township respondents considered this factor to be very important in their housing search. This finding reflects two factors. Firstly, there were few Orthodox families in the sample of movers and thus, most of the families had no reservations about driving outside the community to a synagogue for Sabbath or holiday services. (In Orthodox Judaism it is forbidden to drive on the Sabbath as this is considered a type of work.) Secondly (as we shall see in a later section), most of the respondents limited their housing search to the Wynnefield-Lower Merion Township area; and most locations in this area are highly accessible by car to one or more congregations. Thus, there was little variation within this area in the degree to which locations provided accessibility to synagogues. Since there was so little variation, it would be unlikely that respondents could use this factor as a basis for choosing among different locations.

As anticipated, the concern for the religious composition of the area (as part of the housing search) was a function of the family's Jewish cultural and religious characteristics. More specifically, those with a strict attitude toward intermarriage were far more likely to consider the religious composition of the area as a very important criteria in the housing search than those with lenient attitudes. Parents with a strict attitude were probably concerned that if they moved to a predominantly gentile area there would be an increased possibility that their children would meet and date gentiles. In addition, householders with strict attitudes toward intermarriage probably wanted to restrict their social life to other Jewish families and it would only be possible to do this in an area containing a sizeable number of Jewish families.

6.4.3. Types of areas considered

Table 4 documents the tendency for study area families to focus their housing search on nearby areas and secondarily to limit their housing search to the western section of the city. Lower Merion Township was the area most frequently mentioned by both Wynnefield and Lower Merion Township movers, although it was mentioned somewhat more frequently by members of the latter group.[2] Furthermore, a surprisingly large proportion (one fifth) of the Wynnefield respondents considered relocating within that community. Undoubtedly, most of these families were thinking about moving to the high rise and garden apartments in the northern section of the community. Such a move would insulate them, to a certain degree, from racial change. Firstly, racial change was occurring relatively slowly in the northern section of the community. Secondly, residents of high rise apartments often have little physical or social contact with residents of the surrounding area. Thirdly, by renting they would not have to face the

---

2. We are using the terms Lower Merion Township and the western suburbs interchangeably. The survey results indicated that few of the respondents considered locations in the western suburbs outside Lower Merion Township.

Table 4. Communities considered in selection of new location.

	Proportion of respondents who considered the area	
	Wynnefield (N = 20)	Lower Merion Township (N = 11)
Within city:		
Center City	15%	30%
North Philadelphia	9	0
Northeastern Philadelphia	26	0
Northwestern Philadelphia	11	0
South Philadelphia	0	0
West Philadelphia	10	10
Logan	5	0
Overbrook	11	0
Wynnefield	21	10
Within suburbs:		
New Jersey suburbs	10	18
Northeast suburbs	10	0
Northwest suburbs	5	0
Southwest suburbs	5	18
Western suburbs	40	55

problem of experiencing a loss in equity as a result of declining property values. The crosstabular results provide additional evidence in support of this latter point. The fact that the family moved from the previous location because of racial change (or because of problems with the public schools) was relatively unimportant in predicting whether the family would consider one or more suburban locations. Fifty eight percent (12) of those who felt that racial changes were very important in their moving decision, as compared to 65 percent (17) who felt that they were not very important, considered one or more suburban areas.

There was some support for the hypothesis that the more religiously and culturally identifiable Jewish families would limit their housing search to areas of high Jewish density. One Jewish cultural characteristic – the attitude toward intermarriage – did influence the housing search within Lower Merion Township. Householders with a strict attitude confined their search to southeastern Lower Merion Township, where Jews constituted a large minority of the population. In contrast, those with more lenient attitudes were more likely to extend their search to the northwestern section of the community (where Jews generally constituted a tiny minority). Whereas about two fifths (44 percent, 16) of those who had a lenient attitude toward intermarriage considered one or more of those predominantly non-Jewish communities, only about one fifth (19 percent, 16) who had a strict attitude considered these areas.[3]

The more religiously oriented Jewish families were not more likely to extend their housing search to Northeast Philadelphia, which contains the major Jewish concentration in the Philadelphia area. There were insignificant associations between the likelihood of considering Northeast Philadelphia on the one hand and Jewish religious and cultural characteristics on the other. Perhaps the insignificant results reflect the fact that Northeast Philadelphia is fairly distant from the Wynnefield-Lower Merion area, combined with the fact that families, regardless of their degree of religiosity, were reluctant to move across sectoral boundaries. Furthermore, Northeast Philadelphia is far less accessible to Center City Philadelphia than is the Wynnefield-Lower Merion area.

Why was the attitude toward intermarriage an accurate predictor of where families looked for homes in Lower Merion Township? The explanation here is basically the same as the one presented earlier, regarding the reasons why those with strict attitudes toward intermarriage were more likely to consider the religious composition of areas as a very important criteria in the housing search than those with lenient attitudes. Parents with strict attitudes probably were concerned that if their families moved to predominantly gentile areas in Lower Merion Township, there would be an increased likelihood that their children would meet and date gentiles. In addition, regardless of whether they had children, householders with strict attitudes probably preferred to socialize with other Jewish families. Being in a predominantly gentile area would decrease the possibility for making close Jewish friends in the area.

6.4.4. The evaluation of alternatives

Contrary to what was anticipated, the existence of racial change did not cause families to restrict their housing search, either in terms of time spent in the search or in terms of the number of communities considered. There were relatively small differences between Wynnefield and Lower Merion

3. Communities were categorized into two types: (1) those containing large Jewish minorities; and (2) those containing tiny Jewish minorities, on the basis of the results of the 1969 telephone survey.

movers in terms of the amount of time spent on the search. Sixty percent of the Wynnefield movers (20) as compared to forty percent of the Lower Merion movers (10) spent less than three months in the housing search. Furthermore, there were weak associations between the amount of time spent on the search and both: (1) whether the respondent mentioned racial change as a reason for moving; and (2) the racial composition of the original neighborhood.

There was also no evidence that the existence of racial change caused families to limit the geographical scope of their housing search (that is, the number of communities considered).[4] The mean number of communities considered by Wynnefield families was actually slightly larger than for Lower Merion Township families (3.3 versus 2.3), rather than smaller as was anticipated. Thus, the results provide no support for the stereotype of white families panic moving and taking the first decent home available.

6.4.5. The actual selection of a new location

The results dealing with the actual migration patterns of residents parallel those presented earlier relating to their search patterns. Residents of both Wynnefield and Lower Merion tended to move to nearby areas and secondarily within the western sector of the city.

Table 5 describes the actual locations chosen by families when they moved from their 1969 locations. Figure 1 describes the intercensus tract migration patterns; that is, the movement patterns within the Wynnefield-Lower Merion Township area. Both the table and the figure are based on the sample of Jewish families who completed the 1969 mailed questionnaire and for whom the new address was known. This includes, but is not limited to, those who had completed the 1974 follow-up questionnaire.[5]

As shown, Lower Merion Township was the most common destination of residents of both areas. Figure 1 shows that Wynnefield residents who moved to Lower Merion Township relocated to nearby communities just across the city boundary. Similarly, most of the moves of Lower Merion Township residents were within the communities immediately to the west

4. In order to measure the number of communities considered, a new variable was computed from the results of three items in the survey: (1) the number of Philadelphia communities considered; (2) the number of suburban areas considered (e.g., the western suburbs); and (3) the number of communities considered in the western suburbs.
5. The remainder of this chapter is based on the sample of families who completed both the 1969 and 1974 surveys.

Table 5. Location of new home, by community area, by 1969 location. (Proportions moving to particular areas.)

	Wynnefield	Lower Merion Township
Within City:		
Center City	3%	14%
Northeast	10	0
Northwest	5	4
Wynnefield	20	7
(Subtotal)	(38)	(25)
Within suburbs:		
Northwest	5	0
Southwest	3	3
West-Lower Merion Township	27	45
Other West suburbs	7	3
(Subtotal)	(42)	(51)
Outside Philadelphia Metropolitan area	20	24
	N = 40	N = 29

of Wynnefield. A surprisingly large proportion (20 percent) of Wynnefield movers relocated within that community, given the existence of racial change in that area. As shown in Figure 1 most of these were families who relocated to the apartment area in the Upper Hill section of the community.

Even when Wynnefield families moved because of racial change, this did not increase their likelihood of moving out of the community. This is shown by the fact that respondents who mentioned racial change, or decline in the quality of public schools, as reasons for moving were not more likely to move to suburban areas than respondents who did not consider these reasons to be very important. It appears that many older families who owned their homes adapted to racial changes by moving to apartments a short distance away. In this way, they insulated themselves to a certain degree from racial changes but at the same time were able to maintain familiar patterns and contacts. As we mentioned earlier, these were probably families who would have moved anyway but whose moves were hastened by the existence of racial change.

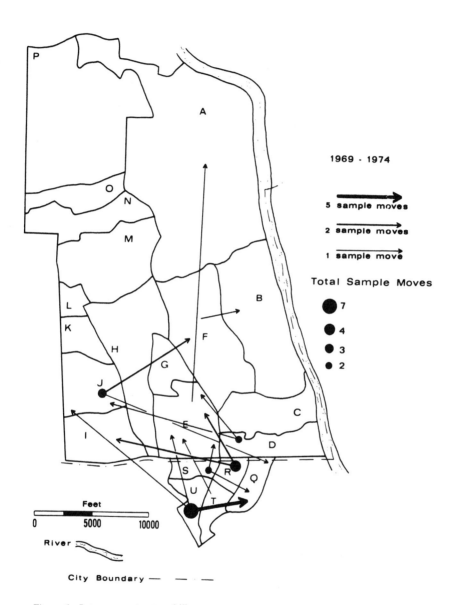

Figure 1. Intercensus tract mobility.

6.5. Conclusions

This chapter has employed reason analysis to study three aspects of the mobility process in a racially changing community: (1) the decision to move; (2) the search for a new residence; and (3) the actual selection of a new home. We have attempted to determine the extent to which these three stages of the process differ between a racially changing and a stable predominantly white community. We have also sought to determine how Jewish religious and cultural characteristics influence these three stages in a racially changing community.

Wynnefield and Lower Merion residents did differ in terms of reasons for moving. Wynnefield residents tended to move because of the existence of racial change and the impacts of racial change on community standards (e.g., declines in the quality of local public schools and local shopping facilities). On the other hand, Lower Merion Township movers emphasized their dissatisfaction with the quality of their own housing conditions (e.g., the layout of the home). The fear of crime was the most frequently mentioned reason for moving among both Wynnefield and Lower Merion Township residents.

The existence of racial change did influence the housing search pattern of Wynnefield residents in one important way. Residents who moved for this reason were particularly concerned about the social composition of prospective new locations. In two other respects, the search for and selection of new homes were remarkably similar among residents of the two communities. Firstly, residents of the two communities spent about the same amount of time in the search and considered about the same number of communities. There was no evidence that the existence of racial change caused Wynnefield residents to restrict their housing search in either of these two ways. Secondly, residents of both communities searched for and selected homes in nearby areas. A surprisingly large number of Wynnefield families relocated within that community.

One Jewish cultural characteristic – the attitude toward intermarriage – played an important role in the decision to move from Wynnefield locations as well as in the search for and selection of a new home. Those with a strict attitude toward intermarriage were more likely to explain their moves as resulting from the decline in the number of Jewish families in the area. In searching for a new house, they were concerned about the religious composition of new locations. As a result, they were more likely to search for and select homes in nearby sections of Lower Merion Township where the density of the Jewish population was relatively high. These results provide additional evidence to that presented in Chapter 5, that ethnic variables influence the decision when to move as well as the decision where to move in racially changing communities.

7. Synagogues and churches in changing communities:
What role can they play in stabilization efforts?

7.1. Introduction

The previous four chapters have examined the characteristics of the racial transition process. In this chapter, the focus shifts to the feasibility of efforts at the community level to achieve stable integrated communities. Since churches and synagogues are among the most important institutions in these communities, it is important that they be involved in stabilization efforts. A key question which has not received much attention by researchers is the extent to which these religious institutions would gain or lose support as a result of participation in such efforts. This chapter will be aimed at closing this gap in existing research.

One specific objective of this chapter will be to examine the level and nature of support for church and synagogue involvement in stabilization efforts (e.g., to attract families to the area, to attempt to improve the quality of local public schools). More specifically, we will attempt to answer the following questions with respect to the role of synagogues in racially changing Jewish communities. What is the degree of support for these types of stabilization programs in comparison to other alternatives that are available (e.g., to relocate the synagogue to newer Jewish concentrations)? What types of members are most likely to support these stabilization programs?

A second objective is to examine the level and nature of support for synagogue involvement in biracial community action. If synagogues (and churches) are to play a meaningful role in stabilization efforts, they will probably have to work through resident associations encompassing all religious and racial segments of the community. Furthermore, it may be desirable for such congregations to open their buildings and programs to the surrounding community (e.g., by opening the gymnasium, if there is one, to residents of the surrounding area). It is uncertain whether support now exists for this type of involvement because of the deterioration in black-Jewish relations since the mid-1960's.

Historically, Jews were in the forefront of the civil rights movement. During the early 1960's, many rabbis participated in the civil rights demonstrations in the American South. This situation changed in the late 1960's and early 1970's when there were a number of black-Jewish confrontations in New York and other cities: (1) the Ocean Hill-Brownsville teachers dispute in Brooklyn, New York (1967-1968; see Berube and Gittel, 1969); (2) the Forest Hills housing crisis (1972; see Cuomo, 1974); (3) the damage to Jewish owned businesses during the urban riots; and (4) the anti-Israel position taken by black militants. These confrontations led to an increasing propensity among Jewish voters to support conservative candidates (Friedman, 1974). This would imply that during this period there was decreased support for synagogue participation in social action, including involvement in stabilization programs. There has been, however, little research on this subject.[1]

This chapter will attempt to answer the following questions regarding support for synagogue involvement in biracial community action. Firstly, what was the level of support for different types of activities? Secondly, what types of householders were most likely to support these types of programs? Thirdly, did respondents tend to become more, or less, interested in these types of programs between 1969 and 1974? Finally, which types of respondents tended to change their attitudes toward these programs?

7.2. Methodology

This chapter utilizes two different samples. We rely on data from the 269 Jewish families who completed the Wave 1 mailed questionnaire in order to examine the determinants of support for synagogue involvement in neighborhood stabilization. We utilize data from the 154 families completing both the Wave 1 and Wave 2 questionnaires in order to examine the determinants of changes in support for synagogue involvement in neighborhood stabilization activities.

---

1. Labovitz (1975: 34) notes that there has been little research on the more general subject of Jewish attitudes toward blacks.

7.3. Hypotheses

7.3.1. Support for synagogue involvement in stabilization efforts

1. *Socio-economic status.* We assumed that young, highly educated and higher income respondents would be more likely to have politically liberal attitudes and consequently, would be most likely to support synagogue involvement in stabilization programs.

2. *Attitude toward Jewish-gentile relationships.* We assumed that Jews who prefer to limit their social contacts to other Jews would be reluctant to have the synagogue involved in efforts which involve relatively close social contacts between Jews and gentiles (e.g., on committees). The survey provided two indicators of the householder's emphasis on Jewish-gentile social relations: the attitude toward intermarriage and the number of gentile friends.[2] We assumed that a strict attitude toward intermarriage and the lack of any gentile friends would be correlated with a low level of support for synagogue involvement in biracial community activities and involvement in neighborhood stabilization policies.

3. *Organizational orientation.* We assumed that householders who were themselves actively involved in Jewish organizational life or actively involved in community organizations would support the synagogue's playing a more active civic role. More specifically, we expected that the following types of families would support this type of synagogue involvement: (a) those that belonged to one or more civic, cultural, fraternal or religious organizations meeting in their community; (b) those that belonged to a relatively large number of Jewish cultural, civic and fraternal organizations; and (c) those that participated in a relatively large number of committees at Beth Zion Temple.

4. *The reality of racial change.* Our hypothesis here was that those faced with the reality of racial change would be most likely to support synagogue involvement in biracial community activities and to support efforts to attract Jewish families to the Wynnefield area. More specifically, we expected that those respondents that lived in predominantly black neighbor-

2. This variable was computed from two separate questions on the survey: the number of friends in the immediate vicinity of the family and the number of friends of the family who lived in the immediate area who were Jewish.

hoods and who expected the proportion of blacks to increase, would be most likely to support synagogue involvement in biracial community activities and efforts to attract Jewish families to the area.

7.3.2. Changes in support for synagogue involvement in biracial community action

Those characteristics which were presumed to influence support for synagogue involvement in biracial community activities were also expected to influence the likelihood of experiencing changes in this attitude. More specifically, we hypothesized that (between 1969 and 1974) young, educated and well-to-do respondents, those sympathetic to Jewish-gentile social relationships, those having an organizational orientation, and those for whom racial change was a reality, were most likely to become more interested in synagogue community involvement.

7.4. Findings

7.4.1. Support for synagogue involvement in stabilization policies

1. Overall level of support

As part of the questionnaire sent to Beth Zion Temple members, respondents were asked about their support for four policies aimed at attracting members to the congregation. Two of the policies may be considered neighborhood stabilization policies: to do more to attract Jewish families to Wynnefield and to help improve schools in the Wynnefield area.

As shown in Table 1, the most strongly supported policy by the congregation is the one which would attract Jewish families to the Radnor area, presumably the Beth Zion branch in Radnor (Radnor is a suburb to the southwest of Wynnefield). The second most popular policy, receiving somewhat less support than the first, would be to attract Jewish families to Wynnefield. (Note the difference of the wording of the two items. The first invokes a synagogue membership campaign and the second an attempt to influence residential movements.) This was supported by about three fourths of the membership. Two slightly less popular policies, but not unpopular, were suggestions to relocate near the largest potential number of members and to help improve the public schools in Wynnefield. Both of these policies were supported by about two thirds of the members. The

Table 1. Proportions of Beth Zion members approving different policies aimed at attracting members.

One of the general options open to Beth Zion Temple in the future is to try to attract new members. A number of policies have been proposed to enable Beth Zion Temple to attract members. Please indicate the extent to which you approve of each of the following alternatives available to Beth Zion Temple.

	Total congregation	Wynnefield*	Lower** Merion
Policies			
Do more to attract unaffiliated Jewish families in the Radnor area*** to the synagogue there.	89%	87%	90%
Do more to attract unaffiliated Jewish families to Wynnefield and the surrounding area.	74	76	71
Relocate the main physical plant to a location most convenient to the largest number of potential members.	67	65	70
Help to improve the public schools in the Wynnefield area.	66	68	66

  * N = 61 approximately.
 ** N = 56 approximately.
*** A suburban community to the southwest of Wynnefield.

relatively low level of support for this latter policy may have reflected the fact that it would require the participation of the synagogue in the political arena and that this would be a step removed from the primary mission of the synagogue.

One might have expected that Wynnefield residents would have been more likely to have supported the two stabilization programs because this would have been in their own interest. Unexpectedly, there were similar levels of support between Wynnefield and Lower Merion residents.

2. Factors affecting support

The scores from the two items dealing with stabilization programs were combined to form a scale score measuring support for synagogue involvement in stabilization efforts.[3] The new variable was regressed with the independent variables listed above. Table 2 shows that the only statistically significant predictor of the level of support for this type of community involvement was the householder's level of involvement in Beth Zion Temple. Those who participated in a relatively large number of activities (e.g., served on committees) were far more likely to support the involvement of the Temple in neighborhood stabilization than those who participated in few of these activities. There was, however, an insignificant correlation between support for this policy and the level of participation in Jewish organizations, other than Beth Zion Temple.

7.4.2. Support for synagogue involvement in biracial community action

1. Overall levels of support

Householders completing the 1969 and 1974 mailed questionnaires were asked three questions relating to their support for synagogue involvement in biracial community action ranging from sponsoring a lecture series to promoting a community development corporation. One policy – sponsoring a lecture series bringing blacks and whites together – was clearly the most popular; being supported by about seven tenths of the respondents (Table 3). The other two policies – opening the synagogue's recreational facilities to all members of the community and becoming actively involved in a community development corporation – were considerably less popular; being supported by about one half of the respondents. The lower levels of support for the latter two policies is not that surprising in that they are considerably more controversial. Respondents may have felt that if the facilities were open to the surrounding community they would be utilized by a predominantly black clientele, and that members would then become

3. The scores for the two separate items ranged from 0 to 3. The combined scores ranged from 0 to 6, with a 6 indicating a high level of support. Based on the initial frequency distribution, we classified those with scores of 4 and above as relatively interested in synagogue participation in stabilization activities. On the basis of this dividing point, two thirds, (67 percent, 38) of the Wynnefield respondents and three fifths of the Lower Merion Township respondents (60 percent, 53) were considered to be relatively interested in this type of policy.

These two items form a Likert-type scale; that is, they provide an indication of the degree of support for synagogue involvement in stabilization strategies.

A disadvantage of these items is that they do not constitute a Guttman scale; that is, several patterns of response to the same items could produce the same score.

Table 2. Results of regression analyses relating attitudes toward community involvement with different personal characteristics for Jewish respondents in Wynnefield and Lower Merion Township.*

	Biracial community action				Stabilization policies****			
	R square change	Unstandardized regression coefficient	Standard error of unstandardized regression coefficient	Standardized regression coefficient	R square change	Unstandardized regression coefficient	Standard error of unstandardized regression coefficient	Standardized regression coefficient
Attitude toward intermarriage	.1648	.2846	.0506	.3912**	.0066	.0888	.4485	.0871
Neighborhood organizational participation	.0097	.2708	.1504	.1198**	***	***	***	***
Income	.0093	−.1539	.0760	−.1562**	***	***	***	***
Neighborhood racial composition	.0059	.0883	.1041	.0717	.0106	−.2026	.1952	−.1174
Number of gentile friends	.0014	−.1138	.2191	−.0355	.0054	.3916	.4485	.0872
Educational level of household head	.0008	.0191	.0451	.0302	.0193	−.1091	.0904	−.1236
Jewish organizational participation	.0006	.0190	.0436	.0298	.0017	.0363	.0890	.0406
Expected racial changes	.0005	−.0483	.1589	−.0223	.0015	.1323	.3245	.0437
Age of household head	.0001	−.0090	.0657	−.0099	.0547	.1840	.1343	.1442

Synagogue membership status	***	***	***	***	
Beth Zion organization participation	----	----	----	----	.0879	.3993	.1336	.2901**
Constant	1.0955			2.8281	
DF	205			100	
R²	.1930			.1875	
F ratio	5.2337**			2.6818**	

* Appendix Table 5A presents the results of the bivariate crosstabular analyses between background characteristics and support for synagogue involvement in neighborhood stabilization activities.
Appendix Table 5B presents the intercorrelations among the variables in this regression analysis.
** F values significant at the .95 confidence level.
*** Variable was included in the regression run but not in the regression equation.
**** This regression analysis is based on data from Beth Zion Temple members only.

Definitions of Variables in Regression Analysis

Biracial Community Action – the extent of support for synagogue involvement in community problems (e.g., opening recreational facilities to all members of the community, categories reflect increasing levels of support for this type of policy); Stabilization Policies – level of support for synagogue involvement in stabilization policies (i.e. attempts to attract unaffiliated Jewish families to the area, attempts to improve the quality of local public schools, categories reflect increasing support for this type of policy); Attitudes toward Intermarriage – degree of tolerance for intermarriage between Jews and gentiles (categories reflect increasing levels of tolerance); Neighborhood Organizational Participation (1) Belong to none, (2) Belong to one or more; Income (categories reflect increasing income levels); Neighborhood Racial Composition (categories reflect increasing proportions of blacks); Gentile Friends (1) Have gentile friends, (2) Have no gentile friends; Educational Level of Household Head (categories reflect increasing education levels); Jewish Organizational Participation – the number of Jewish organizations to which members of the household belong (e.g., Bnai Brith, Hadassah, Sisterhood or Brotherhood of synagogue, categories reflect an increasing number of Jewish organizations); Expected Racial Changes – the proportion of Blacks will: (1) Decrease, (2) Remain the same, (3) Increase; Age of Household Head (categories reflect an increasing number of years); Synagogue Membership Status (1) Not member, (2) Member; Beth Zion Organization Participation – number of Beth Zion activities in which members of the family participate (e.g., clubs, committees, categories reflect an increasing number of activities).

Table 3. 'Proportions of Wynnefield and Lower Merion Township Jews approving different forms of synagogue community involvement.

	Proportion approving	
Activity	Wynnefield*	Lower Merion Township**
Sponsoring a lecture series bringing blacks and whites together	69%	72%
Opening its recreational facilities to all members of the community	47	50
Becoming actively involved in a community corporation promoting housing and employment opportunities for blacks	44	50

* N = 108 approximately
** N = 152 approximately

reluctant to utilize them. Similarly, many might have felt that by becoming involved in a community development corporation the synagogue was getting involved in political action, and that this was too far removed from the primary purposes of the synagogue. There were insignificant differences between Wynnefield and Lower Merion residents in support for these three policies.

2. Factors affecting support

The attitude toward intermarriage is the most important variable in explaining variations in support for synagogue involvement in biracial community activities (Table 2). The significant positive beta coefficient indicates that those who had a lenient attitude toward intermarriage were most likely to support this policy. This finding probably reflects the fact that householders with lenient attitudes were the ones most likely to socialize with gentiles as well as Jews. As a result of their own willingness to interact with gentiles, it is not surprising that they were more likely to support the involvement of the synagogue in activities that would bring Jews and gentiles together.

As anticipated, the organizational orientation of the respondent influenced support for synagogue participation in biracial community activities. Those who belonged to one or more neighborhood based organizations were significantly more likely to support this type of policy than those who did not belong to any such organization. It should be noted, however, that the two measures of participation in Jewish organizations – the synagogue membership status of the family and the number of Jewish organizations to which members of the family belonged – were not accurate predictors of the level of support for this type of policy.

There was no evidence that those living in racially changing communities were more likely to support this policy than those living in stable, predominantly white areas. The weak positive beta coefficient between this attitude and the perceived neighborhood racial composition indicates that those in predominantly white areas were somewhat more interested in this policy, rather than less interested as had been anticipated. Furthermore, there was virtually no correlation at all between support for this type of policy and the expected direction of racial change. These results probably reflect the fact that respondents in the racially changing neighborhoods did not realize that it was in their own interest to support this type of involvement. That is, if there was to be any effective stabilization program it would have been necessary for synagogues to work with all segments of the population, including blacks.

There was also no support for the hypothesized importance of three other variables – age, education and income – in explaining variations in interest for this type of policy. There were insignificant beta coefficients between both age and educational level of the household head and this attitude. Furthermore, there was a significant negative correlation between family income and this attitude, whereas a strong positive correlation had been anticipated.

3. Changes in levels of support between 1969 and 1974

Contrary to expectations, there was no sharp decline in support for synagogue involvement in biracial community action. In fact, almost as large a proportion of the respondents became more interested (25 percent) as became less interested (30 percent).[4] The largest group (45 percent) ex-

---

4. As mentioned, the questions on attitudes toward synagogue involvement in biracial community action were repeated between the 1969 and 1974 questionnaires. In order to compute a measure of change between 1969 and 1974, we subtracted the respondent's score in 1969 from his score in 1974. A negative number means that the respondent became less interested in the subject between 1969 and 1974. A zero means that the respondent's views did not change. A positive score indicates that he became more interested in this type of activity.

Any member of the household could complete the 1969 or 1974 questionnaire. This presented a problem because we were interested in change in attitudes for *particular individuals* during this period. In order to deal with this problem, the analysis in this chapter is limited to those cases where the same individual completed both questionnaires.

perienced no change in their attitudes. This finding is in contrast to the increasing political support provided by Jews for conservative candidates. There is no simple explanation for this discrepancy.

Wynnefield and Lower Merion Township respondents differed significantly with respect to the direction of change in this attitude between 1969 and 1974. Wynnefield respondents were more likely to become more interested while Lower Merion Township respondents were more likely to become less interested (Table 4). The Wynnefield results may reflect the fact that respondents there experienced racial change and were concerned about maintaining a desirable, stably integrated community. They may have felt that if these goals were to be achieved, it would be necessary for the synagogue to become actively involved in community affairs. This greater degree of involvement would almost inevitably imply greater interaction between congregants and their black neighbors.

4. Factors influencing changes in levels of support

Two of the regression results in Table 5 are as anticipated. Firstly, the fact that the respondent lived in a racially changing neighborhood, contributed to the likelihood that he would become more interested in synagogue involvement in biracial community activities. The significant negative beta coefficient between support for this policy and perceptions of the neighborhood's racial composition, means that those who lived in racially mixed neighborhoods (i.e., at least one quarter black) were more likely to become interested in this policy because they became convinced of the importance of neighborhood stabilization policies to maintain the area's racially mixed

Table 4. Relationship between changes in attitudes toward biracial community action and location (1969).

	Location	
Type of change	Wynnefield	Lower Merion Township
Less interest	17	38
Same level of interest	49	42
More interest	34	20
	(35)	(64)

$x^2 = 7.87$
df $= 3$
p $< .05$

Table 5. Results of regression analyses relating changes in attitudes toward biracial community action with different personal characteristics*.

	R square change	Unstandardized regression coefficient	Standard error of unstandardized regression coefficient	Standardized regression coefficient
Attitude toward intermarriage	.0719	—.2057	.1017	—.2546**
Neighborhood racial composition	.0414	—.3020	.1802	—.2234**
Neighborhood organizational participation	.0308	.4329	.2831	.1744**
Jewish organizational participation	.0194	.1219	.0908	.1644**
Number of gentile friends	.0163	—.4858	.4019	—.1497
Age of household head	.0028	.0535	.1287	.0515
Educational level of household head	.0004	—.0137	.0816	—.0192
Family income	.0002	—.0203	.1462	—.0179
Synagogue membership status	.0002	—.0638	.5123	—.0146
Constant	1.6758			
DF	81			
R^2	.1834			
F ratio	1.8217			

* Appendix Table 5C presents the results of the bivariate crosstabular analyses between background characteristics and changes in support for synagogue involvement in biracial community action. Appendix Table 5D presents the intercorrelations among the variables in this regression analysis.
** F values significant at the .95 confidence level.

Definitions of variables in the regression analysis:
Change in Attitudes toward Biracial Community Action-changes in the degree of support for synagogue involvement in biracial community activities (a positive result indicates increased support for this type of policy).
For definitions of the remainder of the variables in the analysis, see Table 2.

character. These residents were probably aware of the fact that if these stabilization efforts were to be successful, they would have to involve all segments of the community, in other words, Jews and blacks.

Secondly, an organizational orientation on the part of the respondent (and other adult members of the household) contributed to the likelihood of an increased level of support for this type of policy. This is shown by the fact that respondents whose households belonged to one or more neighborhood based organizations, were more likely to become interested in synagogue involvement than those in households belonging to no such organization. Similarly, the level of participation in Jewish organizations contributed to the likelihood of becoming more interested in this type of policy.

We had assumed that those with a strict attitude toward intermarriage would become more opposed to synagogue involvement in biracial community activities, but Table 4 provides no support for this assumption. There is a negative beta coefficient between these variables whereas a positive coefficient had been anticipated. The bivariate crosstabular results (Appendix Table 5C) show that those with a relatively strict attitude were more likely to become more interested in this policy during this period than those with a lenient attitude. Whereas 34 percent (53) of those with a strict attitude became more interested, this was only true for 13 percent (40) of those with a lenient attitude. (Interestingly, there were no meaningful differences between those with strict and lenient attitudes in terms of the proportions becoming less interested in this type of policy.) These findings indicate an increasing acceptance, on the part of this type of householder, of the idea of blacks and whites working together around the issue of community betterment. Chapter 5 showed that those with a strict attitude toward intermarriage were more likely to remain in Wynnefield than others, despite the existence of racial change. Because of their stake in the community, they probably were particularly interested in the implementation of effective neighborhood stabilization programs. They probably realized that if these efforts were to be successful, they would have to involve all racial and religious groups.

7.5. Conclusion

This chapter has examined the level and nature of support for synagogue participation in neighborhood stabilization efforts, and the extent to which that support had changed between 1969 and 1974.

There were mixed results with respect to support for synagogue participation in stabilization efforts. On the one hand, members of Beth Zion Temple generally approved of efforts on the part of the congregation to attempt on its own to alter residential patterns. About three fourths supported efforts to attract unaffiliated Jewish families to the Wynnefield area and a similar proportion supported efforts to improve the public schools serving Wynnefield. On the other hand, many Jewish respondents in the Wynnefield-Lower Merion area did not sanction efforts to involve the synagogue in biracial community action. For example, about half were against opening synagogue recreational facilities to the surrounding community. As we have indicated, if locality oriented stabilization efforts are to have any chance for success, they must involve the cooperation of Jews and blacks. The above result suggests there was only limited support for such biracial efforts.

We had expected that as a result of black-Jewish confrontations during the late 1960's and early 1970's, respondents would have become less supportive of synagogue involvement in biracial community action. This was not the case. During the 1969-1974 time period, almost as many respondents became more interested in this policy as became less interested. It is of interest that the attitude toward intermarriage, which was the most important variable in explaining the level of support for biracial community action, was also the most important predictor of changes in support for this policy.

Between 1969 and 1974, those with a strict attitude toward intermarriage were among those most likely to become more interested in synagogue involvement in biracial community activities. This finding probably reflects the fact that this type of family lived in Wynnefield during the late 1960's and early 1970's and became convinced by its experience that black-Jewish cooperation was necessary to maintain the quality of life in the area. This suggests that efforts to stabilize racially changing Jewish communities should focus on these religious families and should try to convince them that it is in their own interest to support the involvement of their synagogue in stabilization efforts involving the total community.

8. Conclusions and policy implications

8.1. Introduction

This chapter has two aims: (1) to review the major findings that have been presented, dealing with the underlying causes of racial transition in Wynnefield; and (2) to examine the implications of these findings for stabilization efforts in racially changing communities.

8.2. Underlying causes of the racial transition process

In order to better understand the underlying causes of transition in Wynnefield, this volume examined factors affecting the move-stay decision of white householders. Five major conclusions may be derived from the analysis.

Firstly, a key factor influencing white moving decisions was the perception that the surrounding neighborhood was undergoing racial change, combined with an unwillingness on the part of whites to be part of a racial minority. Three separate findings supported this conclusion: (1) the fact that Wynnefield whites had more rapid moving plans than whites living in Lower Merion Township; (2) the fact that the respondent's perception of the surrounding neighborhood's racial composition was an important variable in explaining variations in mobility behavior among Jewish Wynnefield residents, i.e., that those living in neighborhoods that were at least one half black were far more likely to move than those living in neighborhoods that still had white majorities; and (3) the fact that the overwhelming majority (62 percent) of Wynnefield residents who moved between 1969 and 1974 (and who completed the Wave 2 mailed questionnaire) mentioned the existence of racial change as a very important reason for moving.

Secondly, the level of racial prejudice was not an accurate predictor of the likelihood of moving among Jewish Wynnefield residents. The fact that the respondent had a positive attitude toward housing or educational integration did not significantly increase the likelihood of his remaining in Wynnefield. This finding reflects the fact that those who said they were interested in residential integration were only interested in living in a racially mixed community if whites were in the majority. The pro-integration sentiments of some Wynnefield residents were irrelevant by 1969 because many of the neighborhoods in Lower Wynnefield had become predominantly black.

Thirdly, the decision to remain in Wynnefield was influenced by the perceived quality of the home. The housetype of the family was a key factor in explaining variations in mobility behavior. Those living in single-family detached homes were far less likely to move than those living in the attached homes or apartments. The detached single-family homes were large, attractive and on shady streets. In contrast, the row houses were small and were viewed as obsolete by most white residents. The detached home residents probably decided to remain because they realized they could not obtain comparable housing values in nearby suburban areas.

Fourthly, the concern about street crime was a major factor in influencing the moving decisions of Wynnefield residents. Nearly all (90 percent) of the Wynnefield movers (who completed the Wave 2 questionnaire) cited crime as being a deciding factor in their move. The fear of crime in Wynnefield was not exaggerated. During the late 1960's and early 1970's, there was a drastic rise in the incidence of violent street crime. A series of stabbings of women and gang violence dramatized the issue.

Finally, the householder's attitude toward Jewish-gentile social relations had an effect on the decision of whether to move as well as on the decision of where to move. A strict attitude toward intermarriage contributed to decisions to remain. This finding probably reflected the strong social bonds among religious families in the area and the fact that these bonds provided an incentive to remain. In addition, this same factor also influenced housing search behavior; those Jews who moved were significantly more likely to be concerned about the religious composition of future locations and were significantly less likely to consider homes in the predominantly non-Jewish sections of Lower Merion Township. In the past, geographers and sociologists have speculated that ethnic variables influence the decision of where to move, but not the decision of whether to move. The above results suggest that in racially changing Jewish communities at least, ethnic variables affect both decisions.

8.3. Policy implications

The volume's findings are suggestive of the types of neighborhood stabilization strategies that are most likely to be effective.

Firstly, *localistic stabilization strategies (those implemented within racially mixed areas) are likely to have limited potential for success.* The Wynnefield Residents Association was the main vehicle for stabilization in that community. The activities it has implemented are typical of those of resident associations in racially changing communities: attempting to improve community morale by organizing block clubs; lobbying for improved city services; participating in the preparation of the master plan for the community; and attempting to limit real estate solicitation.

There is no evidence that these activities had any impact whatsoever on the rate of racial change. Between 1969 and 1970, the community changed from a predominantly white one to a demographically biracial one (about one half black). The Residents Association has been unsuccessful in achieving stabilization because it has been inherently unable to influence those forces responsible for black housing demand being focused on the area (e.g., white suburban prejudice, public and private institutional practices severely limiting the availability of low and moderate income housing to blacks in suburban areas).

Secondly, *metropolitan-wide housing policies aimed at dispersing low and moderate income black families are needed in order to improve the long-range prospects for stabilizing mixed communities.*

A key factor fostering existing patterns of racial transition is the concentration of black demand on mixed areas in proximity to the ghetto (Rose, 1970). Dispersal policies would decrease the pressure of black demand on these mixed communities. Consequently, white residents of these areas would be more optimistic about their communities remaining mixed (rather than becoming predominantly black). Furthermore, those whites who might have wanted to move in order to avoid living in a mixed area, probably would be discouraged from doing so because of the presence of blacks in most suburban communities (Thompson, 1968: 309-18).

It is unlikely that this goal of the dispersal of black and low income housing demand could be achieved simply by eliminating discriminatory barriers. Firstly, little low and moderate income housing is likely to be built in the suburbs because of the rising costs of housing and because of the increasing acceptance of the no-growth philosophy by suburban officials. Secondly, the courts have upheld the right of suburban communities to pass restrictive ordinances which limit the amount of low and moderate-income housing built.[1] Thirdly, even if existing discriminatory barriers were re-

---

1. Two sets of Supreme court decisions—one involving Arlington Heights, Illinois (a Chicago

moved, it is uncertain whether blacks would take advantage of suburban housing opportunities. This point is illustrated by a recent experiment in Kansas City where families were given rent money and told to find housing of their own choice (Bigart, 1972). The families who participated did not 'open up the suburbs'. 'They moved down a corridor of neighborhoods that were already changing from white to black.' Finally, one might question the overall validity of a strategy relying on existing federal laws to remove discriminatory barriers. The United States Civil Rights Commission recently issued a report indicating that the Department of Housing and Urban Development and other federal departments had been ineffective in enforcing laws aimed at banning discrimination in the sale and occupancy of housing (Holsendolph, 1975). There is no reason to believe that the federal government would more effectively enforce these laws in the future than it has in the past.

Ideally, metropolitan-wide housing policies would be implemented along with metropolitan-wide school districts. Many central city school districts are finding that efforts to desegregate their schools are counterproductive because these efforts are leading to a further exodus of whites. As Manley (1976: 587) notes, the only way to approach this problem is on a metropolitan basis:

Past experience has led white families to expect a changing neighborhood to become eventually all black, and consequently, without a neighborhood school that will remain integrated· for a substantial period of time. Metropolitan desegregation would assure people that schools would be integrated and remain integrated no matter where they lived in the metropolitan area.

Movement toward the implementation of metropolitan housing and educational integration policies has been slow. As Delaney (1974) notes, there have been a dozen metropolitan housing plans developed around the

---

suburb) and another involving two New Jersey communities–illustrate this point. In the former, the court ruled that the village had not violated the equal protection provision of the 14th Amendment because it refused to change the provisions of its zoning regulations to permit the construction of a low-income townhouse. The court, thus, reaffirmed the principle that an official policy having a disproportionate impact on one racial group is not unconstitutional unless discrimination can be shown as a motive for the policy (*New York Times,* January 16, 1977).

In 1975, in a case involving Mt. Laurel Township, New Jersey the Supreme Court held that zoning that excluded housing for the poor and moderate-income families violated the constitution and state law. However, in a more recent ruling involving Washington Township and Demarest in Bergen Country, the same court limited the impact of the Mt. Laurel decision to those localities not already built up with single-family homes (Fried, 1977).

country using the fair share concept.[2] Only two, however, Dayton, Ohio and Minneapolis-St. Paul, have been implemented to a significant degree. In Dayton, nearly half of the 14,000 units under the plan have been constructed. In Minneapolis, 9,000 units have been built in the suburbs since the plan was adopted in 1972 (McFall, 1977).

Only two metropolitan school districts have been implemented – Louisville, Kentucky and Wilmington, Delaware – and both were products of court rulings. Suits have been unsuccessful in Detroit and Richmond, Virginia. The former decision is particularly relevant since it might limit the application of this remedy to other metropolitan areas. 'Essentially the Court ruled in (the Detroit) case that metropolitan relief was justified only if it could be shown that both suburban schools and the central school district had engaged in segregation practices' (King, 1977). It would appear that if school segregation was a product of changing housing patterns, then this remedy would not be applicable.

The underlying reason why these two policies have been implemented so slowly is that only a small proportion of Americans is in favor of them. Even among social scientists, there is a sharp debate as to whether a 'ghetto dispersal plus enrichment strategy' or an 'enrichment only strategy' should be adopted by the federal government (see Downs, 1968: 1341-65). It is clear that unless the values of many Americans change – leading to the implementation of such a strategy – the prospects for stabilizing racially changing fringe neighborhoods will remain very much in doubt.

This suggests a third policy implication: *that neighborhood organizations, including churches and synagogues, should advocate for the development and implementation of metropolitan housing and educational policies.* They should do this because these policies would be in their interest, since they would promote the stability of racially changing communities, as well as promote equal housing opportunities. National ethnic organizations (e.g., the American Jewish Committee) should pressure the federal government to require local governments to cooperate through metropolitan planning agencies, in the development and implementation of dispersal policies as a condition for receiving other forms of governmental assistance (e.g., aid for highways). At the local level, synagogues and churches through local residents' associations and city-wide ethnic organizations

2. Under this concept each suburban government agrees to accept a certain percentage of the low and moderate income housing to be built. For a more detailed discussion of the Dayton Plan, see Bertsch and Shafor (1971).

should pressure local governments to cooperate in the development of such metropolitan-wide plans. Precedents already exist for the latter approach. For example, the Jewish Community Relations Council of Philadelphia supported legislation to end redlining (*Jewish Exponent*, August 6, 1976). It would simply be an extension of this type of effort to support metropolitan housing and educational policies.

Fourthly, *localistic stabilization programs could be useful if implemented in conjunction with metropolitan dispersal policies.* The following points should be taken into account in the development of these localistic policies. One would be a focus on attracting new white families as well as on holding existing white residents.

The racial transition process in Wynnefield involved both a reduction in white housing demand as well as a speed-up in white outmigration. Even if there were no speed-up in white outmigration racial change still would have taken place because all, or nearly all, of the homes that would have been put up for sale in the course of normal turnover would have been purchased by blacks. This would imply the need to develop policies aimed specifically at attracting white families to racially mixed areas. Two policies mentioned in the literature, ought to be tested by ethnic organizations: (1) low interest mortgage loans to ethnic families purchasing homes in the area (Council of Jewish Welfare Funds, 1974: 5; Kandell, 1972); and (2) an insurance program against the risk of experiencing a drop in property values (Yarmolinsky, 1971; Williams and Simons, 1977). In addition, stabilization policies should not necessarily focus on attracting the young and educated. Most localistic policies are based on two premises: (1) that changing areas have a greater appeal to young educated households; and (2) that the role of policy is to enhance the attractiveness of these areas for this segment of the population. The results in Chapters 4 and 5 suggest that changing communities do *not* have a greater appeal to the young and educated. Policies aimed at attracting and retaining members of this group will not be successful.

Instead of trying to attract whites with tolerant attitudes, stabilization policies should try to attract whites on the basis of the availability of high quality housing at reasonable cost (assuming that this situation exists). As we have pointed out, the relative stability of the Upper Hill section of Wynnefield was primarily due to the attractiveness of the housing.

Also, community agencies should be honest about the impacts of racial change on community standards. As part of an educational campaign to reduce fears among Wynnefield whites, a Philadelphia Jewish Community

Relations Council report concluded that racial changes were not having an adverse impact on community life. This conclusion was overly optimistic in light of the nature of the transition process in the late 1960's and early 1970's. Perhaps the authors of the report were unaware of the impact of racial change on community standards (e.g., crime rates) in other racially changing communities. It is unlikely, however, that many of the residents were convinced by the report that the transition process would be problem free. Many had either lived in other racially changing communities or knew of others living in such communities. This suggests that in the future, planners should accurately portray to residents the negative impacts that racial change may have on the community and at the same time, develop programs to deal with these problems. If this is to occur, it would be helpful if planners had available the results of case studies such as this one. Furthermore, they should be encouraged to seek the advice of experts at local universities (e.g., city planners, sociologists and geographers) in designing neighborhood stabilization programs.

Finally, community agencies should formulate programs to cope with violent street crimes. Crime was the most serious problem affecting Wynnefield during the late 1960's and early 1970's. Furthermore, as we have noted above, the concern was an important factor influencing the moving decisions of white residents. It is difficult to imagine how stable racial integration can be attained unless the concern is dealt with. Local community agencies possess only a limited ability to deal with this problem because the causes of crime are complex and are societal in origin. The following are two of the things that community organizations have done up to now (Delaney, 1976): (1) pressure the local government for changes in the type of police protection and for better street lighting; and (2) inform residents about crime patrols and block watcher groups. These organizations need to experiment with other approaches and in doing so, will continue to require the financial support of the federal, state and local governments.

In conclusion, synagogue and church participation in localistic stabilization efforts is feasible as long as members are educated as to why such efforts are in their own interests.

The results provide strong evidence of support among synagogue members for efforts on the part of the congregation to alone, try to achieve stable neighborhood integration. There was, however, resistance to efforts to involve the congregation in biracial community action. As we have stressed, cooperation across religious and racial lines is necessary if stabilization efforts are to be successful.

This resistance was particularly strong among the more religious and committed Jewish families. This is a problem because this type of family was most likely to remain in Wynnefield despite the existence of racial change. We would expect similar results in other types of white ethnic communities. That is, there would be a tendency for those who identify most strongly with the ethnic group to be most against working with blacks in community organizations.

The above suggests the need for religious institutions to educate their members on why such biracial community action is necessary. The survey results indicate that such an educational effort could be successful. Between 1969 and 1974, those with a strict attitude toward intermarriage were among those most likely to become more interested in synagogue involvement in biracial community activities. This finding probably reflects the fact that this type of family lived in Wynnefield during the late 1960's and early 1970's and became convinced by its experience that black-Jewish cooperation was necessary to maintain the quality of life in the area.

It is beyond the scope of this volume to provide specific guidelines on how churches and synagogues could convince their members that such cooperation is in their interest. This is a challenge that congregation leaders will have to face since the continued viability of their communities, and in turn, their own institutions, are at stake.

Churches, synagogues and other ethnic institutions (e.g., the parochial schools, youth organizations) could also promote the long-term viability of their own communities through educational programs. These would emphasize the importance of identifiable ethnic communities not only for the immigrant generation but also for its descendants. The intended aim of such efforts would be to increase the likelihood that when these children mature and marry, they will choose to live in a neighborhood occupied by members of their own ethnic group.

These types of public and private efforts might be criticized because white ethnic neighborhoods are perceived to be exclusionary toward blacks.[3] This criticism has some basis in fact. As we noted in earlier chapters, there have been numerous instances when white ethnic com-

3. This issue was raised in the last political campaign when then candidate Jimmy Carter stated that the Federal Government should not take the initiative to change the 'ethnic purity' of some neighborhoods.

munities have physically resisted black inmigration. It should be noted, however, that this resistance is based partly on the fear that the community would undergo complete change. If metropolitan housing dispersal plans could be implemented, these fears might be allayed. Furthermore, there have been examples of identifiable white ethnic communities where whites have coexisted peaceably with blacks. Hamtramck, Michigan is a case in point (Stevens, 1974). This is an identifiable Polish city which is within the city boundaries of Detroit. It would be incorrect to characterize this city as racist.

Blacks have lived here as long as the Poles. The public schools have been integrated for decades and opinion polls have shown blacks to be happy...

Efforts to nurture communities such as Hamtramck or Little Italy in New York City (Fowler, 1976)[4] need to be based on an understanding of the importance of these areas to the economic and social fabric of cities. Monsignor Geno Baroni, a leader in the ethnic movement, and recently appointed Undersecretary of Housing and Urban Development for Neighborhoods, emphasizes this point (Reinhold, 1977a):

If the cities are to be saved from becoming 'black, brown and broke', ethnic diversity must be nurtured... Equity, be it racial, sexual, or economic comes in dealing with those tensions (between groups) honestly. So I am for doing away with the melting pot which tried to level out the difference. The diversity can be a strength.

It will not be a simple matter for planners to resolve the possible conflicts between these two goals of nurturing ethnic areas and preventing exclusion. The important thing is that they at least be aware of this dilemma as they attempt to sustain the central city.

4. A joint proposal of the New York City Planning Commission and the Little Italy Restoration Association sought to bring about a *resorgimento* (resurgence) through (1) zoning regulations aimed at encouraging new restaurants and shops; (2) the reservation of open space for parks; (3) park and sidewalk improvements; and (4) the limitation of new buildings to seven stories.
In Little Italy, ethnic change involves the replacement of Italians by Chinese immigrants.

Appendix 1. Sampling scheme

1.1. Telephone interview survey

The sample was selected from the inverse telephone directory for Phila-delphia and its suburbs – that is, a telephone book listing households by order of their address rather than by alphabetical order. A five percent random sample was selected for Wynnefield and the adjacent southeastern section of Lower Merion Township, and a ten percent sample was drawn for the remainder of Lower Merion Township (the northwestern section). The varying sampling rates were utilized in order to obtain a sufficiently large sample of Jewish families in all parts of the study area to conduct multiva-riate analysis on each sample. The higher sampling rate in the northwestern section of Lower Merion Township reflects the fact that the expected proportion of Jewish families in this section was relatively low.

Telephone interviews were conducted in the summer of 1969 with households in the Wynnefield and southeastern Lower Merion Township samples, and in the early fall of that year with the northwestern Lower Merion Township sample. Introductory letters were sent to potential inter-viewees at the start of the interviewing period, (in the case of the Wynnefield and southeastern Lower Merion Township samples), and sev-eral days prior to the time households were first contacted by telephone (in the case of the northwestern Lower Merion Township sample). These letters bore the names of local clergymen who were familiar with the study, and who were willing to answer questions about it. The letter indicated that the purpose of the study was to contribute to available knowledge about residential settlement patterns, and that the results would be used to assist local civic and religious organizations in improving their services.

Interviewing took place weekday mornings, afternoons and evenings with the primary effort during the evenings. Interviews were conducted only with adult members of the households. The great majority of the interviews were conducted by female college students. Table 1 indicates the record of interviews attempted and completed for these two samples.[1]

1. Appendix 2 discusses the biases introduced by the sampling and interviewing procedures in (1) the telephone interview survey (1969); (2) the wave 1 mailed questionnaire (1969); and (3) wave 2 mailed questionnaire (1974).

1.2. Wave 1 mailed questionnaire

Two separate samples were sent the self-administered questionnaires. The first was a sample of Jewish families who were previously telephone interviewed (to be referred to from here on as the Jewish sample). The second was a sample of members of the congregation that sponsored the original study (to be referred to as the synagogue sample).

Using a table of random numbers, a two thirds random sample was drawn of all the Jewish families telephone interviewed in the Wynnefield and southeastern Lower Merion Township areas (exclusive of members of the congregation sponsoring the study).[2] In northwestern Lower Merion Township, all Jewish families who were telephone interviewed were considered part of the mailed questionnaire sample.

Appendix Table 1A. Proportions of Wynnefield and Lower Merion Township telephone samples interviewed*.

	Wynnefield & Southeast Lower Merion Township		Northwest Lower Merion Township	
	No.	Percent	No.	Percent
Interviewed	475	52	468	53
Not available*	251	28	268	30
Refusals	179	20	152	17
	905	100	888	100

* After three attempts.

A table of random numbers was also used to select 200 families from the 1967-8 membership list of the synagogue sponsoring the study. This list included a total of 1574 families. The list excluded those who had been telephone interviewed, or who had completed the pilot version of the mailed questionnaire. Six families, who had resigned since the membership

2. Congregation members were excluded because it would have been necessary to prepare a special mailed questionnaire for this group. The questionnaire would have been similar to that sent to members of the synagogue sample in including questions on participation in synagogue activities, but would have differed by omitting a printed version of the telephone interview schedule. As a result of the exclusion of about forty congregation members, it is likely that the mailed questionnaire sample is not representative of the Jewish population in Wynnefield and Lower Merion Township.

list had been prepared, were deleted. The sample of 194 families represented a 12% sample of the total membership.

A packet of materials was sent to those who had been selected to be part of the two mailed questionnaire samples. Each packet contained a letter explaining the purpose of the study, the questionnaire itself, and a stamped return addressed envelope for the completed questionnaire. The letter contained a list of rabbis in the area who knew about the study and who were prepared to answer questions about it.

Approximately three weeks after the initial mailing, letters were sent to nonrespondents. Two weeks later the first telephone follow-up to non-respondents was conducted by female staff members. Additional questionnaires were sent, if requested, and the reasons for refusals were noted. The next follow-up occurred three weeks later when the project director made arrangements to deliver and pick up questionnaires at respondents' homes. The project director administered the questionnaire as an interview schedule to several respondents who encountered difficulty in completing it themselves.

In northwestern Lower Merion Township, the schedule for delivering and collecting the questionnaires was concentrated into a two week period. All questionnaires were delivered to the respondents' homes and collected by staff members. Appendix Table 1B shows the record of questionnaires completed as compared to the numbers sent out for each sample. In order to

Appendix Table 1B. Proportions of synagogue sample and total Jewish sample completing and not completing mailed questionnaire.

	Synagogue sample	Total Jewish sample		
		Wynnefield	Southeast Lower Merion Township	Northwest Lower Merion Township
Completed questionnaire	66	56	62	51
Respondents not found	2	16	22	41
Refusals	19	17	16	8
Ineligible*	13	11	0	0
	(194)	(82)	(82)	(84)

* The ineligible families in Wynnefield were those who no longer lived in the area at the time the questionnaires were sent out. The ineligible families in the synagogue sample were those who were no longer members of the congregation.

increase the sample size (to permit multivariate analysis), the total Jewish and synagogue samples are combined in the tables in Chapters 5-7.

1.3. Wave 2 mailed questionnaire

In early June, 1974, follow-up mailed questionnaires were sent to all 269 Jewish families who had completed mailed questionnaires in 1969. When they were returned by the post office with no forwarding address, efforts were made to trace the family's new location using such means as synagogue membership lists. When the new location was found, the family was sent a questionnaire. Two weeks after the questionnaires were sent out, all non-respondents were telephoned to urge a quick return of the questionnaire, to answer questions about the survey and to give assistance in filling it out. During the first week in July, attempts were made to telephone interview the remaining non-respondents (who could be reached by phone) with an abbreviated version of the questionnaire. Appendix Table 1C shows the response rates broken down by location.

Appendix Table 1C. Response status of families sent Wave 2 mailed questionnaires.

| Response status** | Location (1969) | | | |
	Wynnefield	Southeast Lower Merion Township	Northwest Lower Merion Township	Other locations*
Returned questionnaire	60%	64%	65%	46%
Not reached	30	26	33	50
Refused	9	9	2	4
Deceased	1	1	0	0
	(89)	(112)	(43)	(22)

 * This sample consists of members of the synagogue sample that lived outside the study area.
** These four categories total 266 families. An additional three families were not sent questionnaires because cards containing the households' names and addresses were either lost or misfiled.

Appendix 2. Biases introduced by sampling and interviewing procedures

2.1. The telephone interview survey

The sampling and interviewing procedures used in the telephone survey may have introduced several biases. Some of the biases may be associated with the use of an inverse telephone listing as a sampling frame. The presence or absence of a telephone, as well as the number of telephones at a particular residence, is likely to be related to the socio-economic status of the family. However, this was not a particularly serious problem in this study, since the number of families in the lower income brackets was relatively small.

Another bias may arise from the possibility that some income or ethnic groups may be more likely to have unlisted telephones. The lack of time and staff prevented an analysis of the significance of this potential bias as part of the study.

A third possible bias may have been introduced by the fact that when the samples were drawn, the inverse telephone directory that was used had not been revised in the previous two months. As a result, new arrivals into the area may have been underrepresented in the sample. The first step in testing for this potential bias was to identify those households which could not be reached in the course of telephone interviewing, because of a disconnected telephone. One possible reason for reaching disconnected numbers was that the families had moved. Eight percent of the sample drawn in Wynnefield-southeastern Lower Merion Township and 5 percent of the sample in northwestern Lower Merion Township could not be reached, because their telephones had been disconnected. Attempts were made to conduct person-to-person interviews with all households living at addresses having disconnected phones in the Wynnefield-southeastern Lower Merion section, and, due to budgetary limitations, with a 20% sample of such cases in northwestern Lower Merion Township. Too few interviews were completed with households at addresses identified as having disconnected telephones to determine whether there were any statistically significant differences between very recent arrivals and the sample who completed telephone interviews.

A bias may also have been introduced by the possibility that those who could not be reached for interviews (refusals, not at home after repeated call backs) differed significantly from those who were telephone interviewed. Person-to-person interviews were sought with a sample of families who had refused to be telephone interviewed. Due to the fact that a limited number of interviews were completed with previous 'refusers', it was not possible to determine the extent to which a bias was introduced.

Finally, the results may have been biased by the 'vacation effect'; that is, the fact that many of the interviews were conducted during the summer, combined with the fact that higher income families would be more likely to be away during this period. In order to measure the seriousness of this problem, interviews were sought with those who could not be reached, several weeks after the main interviewing period had been completed. In fact, those who were interviewed during the main interviewing period did have lower incomes than those who were interviewed after the main interviewing period was over. One third (35 percent, 722) of those interviewed during the main interviewing period had incomes of $ 15,000 or more. In contrast, nearly two thirds of those interviewed later (64 percent, 63) had such high incomes ($x^2 = 21.0$, df = 1, p<.001). Thus, the telephone interview results tended to underrepresent higher income families in the sample.

2.2. Wave 1 mailed questionnaire

A potential bias, that may have resulted from the administration of the mailed questionnaires, is that those who returned the questionnaire may have differed from those who failed to return it. In order to determine the magnitude of this bias, Appendix Table 2A compares the samples that did, and did not, return the mailed questionnaire with respect to four demographic characteristics – age, length of residence at current location, housetype, and religious denominational affiliation. All four characteristics presumably would affect the likelihood of returning a self-administered questionnaire.

As anticipated, the sample of families not returning a questionnaire contained a disproportionately large number of elderly households. In contrast to what had been anticipated, the sample of nonrespondents

Appendix Table 2A. Comparison of families returning and not returning Wave 1 questionnaire.

	Did return questionnaire	Did not return questionnaire
Age		
Prop. 60 and over	19% (135)	32% (164)*
Length of residence		
Prop. living at address less than 10 years	44% (87)	51% (102)
Housetype		
Prop. living in apartments	15% (142)	20% (170)
Religious denominational affiliation	24% (137)	19% (170)*

* Results statistically significant at the .05 level.

contained disproportionately few Jews who identified with no particular denomination. We had assumed that this type of family would have relatively little interest in a study of Jewish cultural patterns and, consequently, that a disproportionately large number of this type of family would appear in the sample of nonrespondents. As shown, the samples returning and not returning the questionnaires did not significantly differ with respect to the other two characteristics – length of residence and housetype.

The above results suggest that the findings from the mailed questionnaires cannot be generalized to the sample of Jewish families telephone interviewed. This is not a serious problem in this volume since our approach is primarily explanatory rather than descriptive. That is, we focus on the relationships between variables rather than the extent to which any particular characteristic exists in the population. In explanatory analysis, the repesentativeness of the sample is not important.

2.3. Wave 2 mailed questionnaire

Previous studies have indicated that those who participate in the second and later stages of panel studies often differ systematically from those who participate in the first stage. Appendix Table 2B tests for the existence of this problem by comparing the samples returning and not returning the Wave 2 mailed questionnaires with respect to five personal characteristics that might affect the likelihood of continued participation in a study such as this one. As shown, these two samples do differ systematically with respect

Appendix Table 2B. Comparisons of families returning and not returning Wave 2 questionnaire.

Background characteristic	Did return questionnaire	Did not return questionnaire
Age Prop. 61 and over	26% (108)	17% (145)
Educational level Prop. not college grads.	44% (149)	59% (111)*
Housetype Prop. living in apartments	27% (117)	15% (149)*
Mobility Prop. moving between 1969 and 1974	27% (151)	47% (66)*
Religious denominational affiliation Prop. having no specific denom. affiliation	14% (151)	10% (116)

* Results statistically significant at the .05 level.

to three of these characteristics – educational level, housetype and mobility. The sample returning the questionnaire tended to be better educated, was more likely to live in a detached or attached home (rather than an apartment) and was far less likely to have moved between 1969 and 1974. The latter result (i.e., dealing with residential mobility) is really not that surprising. Some of the families who moved between 1969 and 1974 may not have had the questionnaire forwarded to them by the post office. It only forwards mail one year after a family has moved. Secondly, some who moved away from the Wynnefield-Lower Merion Township area may not have returned it because the study had little relevance to them at their new location. These results indicate that there were systematic differences between those who participated in the first and second waves of the study. This means that the results based on the sample of 154 families completing both waves cannot necessarily be generalized to the sample of 269 families surveyed in 1969. As noted above, this is not too serious a problem for this study since our focus is explanatory rather than descriptive.

Appendix 3. Additional statistical analyses for chapter four, determinants of moving plans

Appendix Table 3A. Results of crosstabular analyses relating moving plans (likelihood of moving) with location and personal characteristics for white respondents in the study area as a whole.

	Sample size	% remaining below 3 years	Q values
Age of household head			
below 41	183	27	.54**
41 and over	618	10	
Life cycle position			
40 and under, no children	45	51	.38* **
40 and under, children	138	20	
41 and above, children	203	9	
41 and above, no children	415	10	
Location			
Wynnefield	155	30	.58**
Lower Merion Twp.	693	10	
Likelihood of job transfer			
Expect to be transferred	96	25	.41**
Do not expect to be transferred	702	12	
Tenant status			
Rent	203	27	.55**
Own	637	10	
Children under 6			
1 or more	141	16	.13
None	707	13	
Religious affiliation			
Jewish			
Family is Jewish	312	19	.31**
Family is not Jewish	536	11	
Catholic			
Family is not Catholic	657	14	.09
Family is Catholic	191	12	
Protestant			
Family is not Protestant	535	16	.33**
Family is Protestant	313	9	
Length of Residence			
Below 3 years	248	22	.42**
3 or more years	600	10	
Neighborhood organizational participation			
Belong to one or more	343	11	—.19
Belong to none	502	15	

	Sample size	% remaining below 3 years	Q values
Children 6 to 17			
One or more	294	11	—.21**
None	554	15	
Housetype			
Attached or apartment	316	23	.57**
Detached	530	8	
Family income			
Below $10,000	179	17	.17
$10,000 or more	466	13	
Education			
Less than B.A.	393	15	.13
B.A. or higher	433	12	

* This statistic, the gamma value, is used here because the independent variable consists of more than two categories. The gamma value and the Q value are comparable. Therefore, the results for this variable can be compared with the results for the other variables in this table.
** The Q values or the gamma value is statistically significant at the .95 level of confidence.

Appendix Table 3B. Results of crosstabular analyses relating moving plans (likelihood of moving) with selected personal characteristics for white respondents in Wynnefield and Lower Merion Township.

	Wynnefield			Lower Merion Township		
	Sample size	% Re-maining below 3 years	Q value	Sample size	% Re-maining below 3 years	Q value
Age of household head						
Below 41	35	60	.68**	148	20	.51**
41 and over	113	22		505	7	
Life cycle position						
40 and under, no children	16	56	.54* **	29	48	.36* **
40 and under, children	19	63		119	13	
41 and over, children	23	30		180	7	
41 and over, no children	90	20		325	8	
Children 6 to 17						
1 or more	33	33	.11	261	8	—.21
None	122	29		432	11	
Education						
Less than B.A.	105	30	—.11	288	10	.02
B.A. or higher	44	34		389	10	
Housetype						
Attached, apartment	132	33	.53**	184	17	.43
Detached	23	13		507	8	
Religious affiliation Jewish						
Family is Jewish	128	28	—.20	184	12	.14
Family is not Jewish	27	37		509	9	
Catholic						
Family is not Catholic	139	30	—.04	518	10	—.02
Family is Catholic	16	31		175	10	
Protestant						
Family is not Protestant	147	29	—.18	388	11	.18
Family is Protestant	8	38		305	8	
Length of Residence						
Below 3 years	48	35	.19	200	19	.53**
3 years or more	107	27		493	7	
Neighborhood organizational participation						
Belong to 1 or more	63	24	—.24	280	8	—.17
Belong to none	92	34		410	11	
Children under 6						
1 or more	22	46	.38	119	11	.06
None	133	27		574	10	
Likelihood of job transfer						
Expect to be transferred	10	70	.73**	86	20	.46**
Do not expect to be transferred	144	27		558	8	

	Wynnefield			Lower Merion Township		
	Sample size	% Re-maining below 3 years	Q value	Sample size	% Re-maining below 3 years	Q value
Tenant status						
Rent	46	37	.23	157	24	.65**
Own	108	27		529	6	
Family income						
Below $10,000	59	27	—.12	120	13	.11
$10,000 or higher	56	32		410	10	

Notes: See Appendix Table 3A.

Appendix Table 3C. Inter-correlations of independent and dependent variables for total sample of white respondents, Wynnefield and Lower Merion Township.

	2	3	4	5	6	7	8	9	10	11	12	13	14	15
1	.23	−.10	−.10	−.31	.04	.01	−.02	−.06	.48	−.19	−.05	−.17	.11	−.03
2		−.29	−.28	.18	−.06	.00	−.09	−.31	.35	−.21	.07	−.07	.13	−.13
3			.56	.14	.22	−.02	.19	.44	−.09	.28	.14	.02	.11	.47
4				.34	.21	.04	.17	.26	.01	.07	−.03	.03	−.05	.06
5					.10	.08	.09	−.10	.44	−.22	.10	−.01	.12	.01
6						.12	.06	.09	.23	.01	.11	−.02	.10	.22
7							−.05	.03	.16	−.12	−.15	−.02	−.11	−.08
8								.24	−.03	.14	−.05	−.09	.03	.00
9									−.19	.50	−.09	−.16	.04	.32
10										−.33	.02	−.13	.16	−.05
11											.05	−.15	.14	.22
12												−.41	−.58	−.45
13													−.41	.14
14														.31
15														

Key: 1. Children under 6
2. Children 6 to 17
3. Housetype
4. Tenant status
5. Length of residence
6. Moving plans
7. Likelihood of job transfer
8. Neighborhood organizational participation
9. Family income
10. Age of household head
11. Educational level of household head
12. Jewish
13. Catholic
14. Protestant
15. Location

For definitions of variables see Table 1, Chapter 4.

Appendix Table 3D. Inter-correlations of independent and dependent variables for white Wynnefield respondents.

	2	3	4	5	6	7	8	9	10	11	12	13	14
1	.24	.07	.02	.22	.14	.12	.00	-.04	.42	-.22	-.30	-.29	-.16
2		-.18	-.24	.18	.04	-.01	-.02	-.34	.23	-.23	-.09	-.13	.05
3			.15	-.01	.15	.04	-.02	.27	.06	.00	-.10	-.08	-.01
4				.48	.10	.18	.16	.05	.26	-.13	-.11	-.06	-.10
5					.02	-.19	.10	-.08	.33	-.31	-.04	.01	-.08
6						.23	.11	-.05	.40	-.05	-.07	-.01	-.04
7							.00	.00	.20	-.23	-.16	-.08	-.06
8								.20	.02	.05	-.07	-.06	-.01
9									-.26	-.53	-.04	-.06	.01
10										.46	-.29	-.17	-.21
11											.16	-.01	.22
12												.74	.51
13													-.08
14													

Key:
1. Children under 6
2. Children 6 to 17
3. Housetype
4. Tenant status
5. Length of residence
6. Moving plans
7. Likelihood of job transfer
8. Neighborhood organizational participation
9. Family income
10. Age of household head
11. Educational level of household head
12. Jewish
13. Catholic
14. Protestant

For definitions of variables see Table 1, Chapter 4.

Appendix Table 3E. Inter-correlations of independent and dependent variables for white Lower Merion Township respondents.

	1	2	3	4	5	6	7	8	9	10	11	12	13	14
1		.22	-.12	-.13	.33	.01	-.01	-.03	-.05	.50	-.18	.01	-.16	.16
2			-.27	-.28	.18	-.05	-.01	-.11	-.28	.38	-.18	.19	-.04	.20
3				.71	.19	.14	.02	.24	.36	-.11	.25	-.09	-.05	-.04
4					.30	.24	.03	.18	.29	-.07	.12	-.06	.04	-.07
5						.14	.06	.09	-.14	.48	-.20	.15	-.01	.16
6							.13	.05	.04	.19	-.04	.04	-.01	.05
7								-.06	.07	.15	-.08	-.12	.00	-.10
8									.25	-.04	.17	-.05	-.10	.04
9										-.16	.45	-.32	-.24	-.07
10											-.30	.14	-.11	.24
11												-.11	-.22	.06
12													-.35	-.53
13														-.52
14														

Key: See Appendix Table 3D.

Appendix Table 3F. Results of crosstabular analyses relating moving plans (likelihood of moving) with Jewish cultural characteristics for Jewish Wynnefield residents.

	Sample size	% remaining below 3 years	Q value or gamma value
Non-denominational Jew			
No	82	24	—.27
Yes	47	36	
Orthodox Jew			
No	112	30	.34
Yes	17	18	
Conservative Jew			
No	78	31	.13
Yes	51	26	
Reform Jew			
No	115	29	.00
Yes	14	29	
Synagogue attendance			
Once a month or less	60	25	—.08
More than once a month	41	22	

Appendix Table 3G. Inter-correlations of independent and dependent variables for Jewish Wynnefield respondents.

	1	2	3	4	5	6	7	8	9	10	11	12	13	14	15	16
1		.18	.07	-.02	.23	.09	.18	.00	-.07	.40	-.29	-.15	-.03	.15	.02	-.10
2			-.21	-.21	.21	-.01	-.02	-.02	-.39	.33	-.30	-.12	.08	.00	.11	.06
3				.18	.02	.19	-.10	.00	.28	.10	-.01	.06	.01	.03	-.15	.11
4					.49	.07	-.10	.00	.00	.12	-.05	-.11	.13	.11	-.12	.23
5						-.06	.12	.12	-.05	.30	-.26	-.07	-.02	.12	-.06	.08
6							.11	.10	-.03	.34	-.03	-.13	.10	.06	.00	.09
7							.18	.12	-.03	.08	-.13	-.14	-.13	.18	.08	-.19
8								-.04	.17	-.03	.07	.08	-.01	-.08	.01	.16
9										-.37	.57	.17	-.27	-.03	.07	-.13
10											-.47	-.10	.17	.01	-.04	-.20
11												.25	-.14	-.24	.14	-.05
12													.29	-.61	-.26	.05
13														-.32	-.14	.24
14															-.28	-.07
15																-.27

Key: 1. Children under 6
      2. Children 6 to 17
      3. Housing type
      4. Tenant status
      5. Length of residence
      6. Moving plans
      7. Likelihood of job transfer
      8. Neighborhood organizational participation

      9. Family income
     10. Age
     11. Education
     12. Non-denominational Jew
     13. Orthodox Jew
     14. Conservative Jew
     15. Reform Jew
     16. Synagogue attendance

For definitions of variables see Table 3, Chapter 4.

Appendix 4. Additional statistical analyses for chapter five, determinants of mobility

Appendix Table 4A. Tests for reproducibility and scalability of sets of items included in the regression analysis*.

Tests	Inter-marriage	Driving on the Sabbath	Housing** integration	Educational** integration	Jewish customs
Coefficient of reproducibility	.9524	.9814	.9751	.9749	.9083
Coefficient of scalability	.8300	.9048	.9115	.8529	.5868

* These tests were conducted using the Guttman Scale subprogram in the SPSS package.
** Initially, there were four possible response categories for the items that made up this scale: very against, somewhat against, somewhat interested and very interested. The tests for scalability and reproducibility required that these four categories be combined into two broader groups: against or interested.

Appendix Table 4B. Results of crosstabular analyses relating moving plans (likelihood of moving) and mobility (likelihood of moving) with personal characteristics for Jewish residents of Wynnefield.

	Moving plans			Mobility behavior		
	Sample size	% planning to remain below 3 yrs.	Q value	Sample size	% moving by 1974	Q value
Age of household head						
Below 41	21	29	.28	14	64	.33
41 and above	81	19		65	48	
Life cycle position						
40 and under, no children	14	14	.01*	8	38	.03*
40 and under, children	18	22		14	64	
41 and above, children	25	20		20	45	
41 and above, no children	56	18		45	49	
Children under 6						
1 or more	22	23	.16	18	61	.29
None	91	18		69	46	
Children 6 to 17						
1 or more	32	16	—.14	27	52	.07
None	81	20		60	48	
Tenant status						
Rent	33	21	09	24	46	—.11
Own	76	18		60	52	
Housetype						
Attached, apartment	77	21	.31	59	56	.48**
Detached	33	12		26	31	
Length of residence						
Below 3 years	35	20	.07	24	58	.24
3 or more years	78	18		63	46	
Family income						
Below $10,000	25	24	.33	19	58	.20
$10,000 or more	66	14		52	48	
Education						
Less than B.A.	66	23	.26	51	49	.02
B.A. or higher	41	15		32	50	
Likelihood of job transfer						
Expect to be transferred	15	20	—.04	13	39	—.30
Expect not to be transferred	85	21		63	54	
Neighborhood organizational participation						
Belong to one or more	54	17	—.12	46	46	—.16
Belong to none	59	20		41	54	
Friends in vicinity						
Four or more	49	14	—.20	40	43	—.30
Three or less	60	20		45	58	
Relatives in vicinity						
Some	46	24	.38	33	42	—.21
None	65	12		53	53	

Appendix Table 4B. Continued

	Moving plans			Mobility behavior		
	Sample size	% planning to remain below 3 yrs.	Q value	Sample size	% moving by 1974	Q value
Attitude toward housing integration						
Opposed	34	21	.05	24	58	.30
In favor	63	19		51	43	
Attitude toward educational integration						
Opposed	35	11	—.42	27	52	.10
In favor	63	24		49	47	
Proportion of whites						
Below 75%	44	23	.23	35	63	.39
75% or higher	64	16		49	43	
Expectations of racial change (Proportion of blacks will):						
Increase	88	17	.05	72	53	.34
Remain the same or decrease	19	16		14	36	
Proportion of Jews						
Below 50%	70	20	.17	54	54	.20
50% or higher	40	15		32	44	
Change in neighborhood religious composition (Proportion of Jews will):						
Decrease	75	19	.05	61	56	.38
Remain same or increase	35	17		25	36	
Change in property values (Values will):						
Decrease	33	21	.18	27	63	.31
Remain same or increase	72	15		55	47	
Income contextual position Family income higher than						
neighborhood	55	16	—.01	45	51	.07
Family income equal or lower than neighborhood	30	17		21	48	
Change in income (Typical income will):						
Decrease	32	19	.05	24	58	.21
Remain same or increase	75	17		61	48	
Time to work vs. preferences (Commuting Time):						
Exceeds maximum specified	20	10	—.44	14	43	—.18
Is equal to or less than maximum specified	77	22		60	52	

Appendix Table 4B. Continued

	Moving plans			Mobility behavior		
	Sample size	% planning to remain below 3 yrs.	Q value	Sample size	% moving by 1974	Q value
Satisfaction with commuting						
Relatively dissatisfied	52	19	.07	36	50	.08
Relatively satisfied	41	17		37	36	
Satisfaction with neigh. shopping						
Relatively dissatisfied	57	19	.09	48	52	.18
Relatively satisfied	48	17		35	43	
Jewish denominational affiliation						
Non-denominational Jew						
No	95	13	—.74**	72	49	—.09
Yes	18	50		15	53	
Orthodox Jew						
No	109	19	1.0**	85	48	−1.00**
Yes	4	0		2	100	
Conservative Jew						
No	31	36	.60**	23	48	—.04
Yes	82	12		64	50	
Reform Jew						
No	105	18	—.20	82	51	.62**
Yes	8	25		5	20	
Synagogue attendance						
Once a month or less	56	16	−.06	42	52	.05
More than once a month	34	18		26	50	
Observance of Jewish customs						
Low	58	21	.24	39	46	—.17
High	51	14		44	55	
Attitude toward intermarriage						
Disapprove	66	14	—.40	55	51	—.05
Approve	37	27		28	54	
Attitude toward driving to the Synagogue on the Sabbath						
Approve	49	18	.05	38	45	—.28
Disapprove	53	17		39	49	
Moving plans (plan to remain):						
Below 3 years				14	71	.50**
3 years or more				73	45	

* This statistic, the gamma value, is used here because the independent variable consists of more than two categories. The gamma value and the Q value are comparable. Therefore, the results for this variable can be compared with the results for the other variables in this table.
** The Q value is statistically significant at the .95 confidence level.

Appendix Table 4C. Inter-correlations of variables in regression analysis.

	X_1	X_2	X_3	X_4	X_5	X_6*	X_7
X_1		—.18	—.02	—.27	—.25	.19	.13
X_2			—.19	.26	.09	.10	.23
X_3				—.15	.05	—.14	.05
X_4					.25	.11	.26
X_5						—.20	.07
X_6							.19

Key:

X_1 Age of household head
X_2 Housetype
X_3 Number of relatives in vicinity
X_4 Proportion of whites in neighborhood
X_5 Attitude toward intermarriage
X_6 Moving plans
X_7 Mobility behavior

* The method for coding moving plans for this table differs from the method used for Table 1, page 94. Consequently, the findings are not comparable between the two tables.

Appendix 5. Additional statistical analyses for chapter seven, attitudes toward synagogue involvement in neighborhood stabilization efforts

Appendix Table 5A. Relationships between background characteristics and attitudes toward community involvement and neighborhood stabilization.

Background characteristics	Synagogue community involvement			Neighborhood stabilization activities		
	Sample size	% approving comm. inv.	Q value	Sample size	% relatively interested	Q value
Age						
40 or under	52	67	—.25	21	38	.56*
41 and above	188	55		86	69	
Education						
Below B.A.	127	54	.10	55	69	—.25
B.A. or higher	120	59		54	57	
Income						
Below $10,000	29	59	.00	7	86	—.56*
$10,000 and above	182	59		95	63	
Attitude toward intermarriage						
Relatively strict	141	48	.47*	77	65	—.05
Relatively lenient	95	72		32	63	
Number of gentile friends						
No gentile friends	205	55	.35*	11	36	.56*
One or more gentile friends	35	71		97	67	
Perceived neighborhood racial composition						
Below 75 percent white	42	45	.28	15	87	—.63*
75 percent or more white	206	60		95	60	
Expected racial changes (Proportion of blacks will):						
Decrease-remain same	110	58	—.05	48	54	.38*
Increase	133	56		62	73	
Synagogue membership						
Not a member	25	60	—.07			
Is a member	227	56				
Neighborhood org. part.						
None	134	53	.17	47	62	.08
One or more	119	61		64	66	
Jewish org. part.						
None	36	58	—.01	7	57	—.14
One or more	215	55		103	64	
Beth Zion org. part.						
Low	80	48	.17	72	57	.41*
High	41	56		38	76	

* Q value significant at .95 confidence level.

Appendix Table 5B. Inter-correlations of independent and dependent variables in regression analyses of determinants of attitudes toward synagogue involvement in biracial community activities and efforts to attract Jewish families to the Wynnefield area.

	1	2	3	4	5	6	7	8	9	10	11	12	13
1		.28	−.09	.06	−.05	.41	−.13	.11	−.04	.09	−.03	−.06	.07
2			.24	−.19	−.14	−.05	.12	−.22	.19	.09	.08	−.06	.30
3				−.33	−.19	−.18	.20	−.25	.28	−.01	.13	−.06	.01
4					.33	.14	−.12	.27	−.12	−.01	−.03	−.04	.07
5						.07	−.04	.51	−.19	.19	.17	.14	−.01
6							−.27	.21	−.05	−.02	−.14	−.19	−.13
7								−.05	.14	.07	.15	.10	−.01
8									.42	.10	.17	.04	−.13
9										.06	.02	−.07	.13
10											.17	.17	.28
11												.30	.12
12													.10

Key:
1. Synagogue involvement in biracial comm. activities
2. Synagogue efforts to attract Jews
3. Age of household head
4. Educational level
5. Family income
6. Attitude toward intermarriage
7. Number of gentile friends
8. Neighborhood racial composition
9. Expectation of racial change
10. Community organizational participation
11. Jewish organizational participation
12. Synagogue membership status
13. Beth Zion Temple organizational participation

For definitions of variables, See Table 2, Chapter 7.

Appendix Table 5C. Relationships between background characteristics and the likelihood of becoming more/less interested in biracial community action between 1969 and 1974.

Background characteristics	Sample size	Become more interested		Become less interested	
		% becoming more interested	Q value	% becoming less interested	Q value
Age					
40 and under	26	12	.52*	31	—.03
41 and above	69	29		32	
Education					
Below B.A.	46	28	—.19	28	—.10
B.A. or higher	52	21		33	
Income					
Below $10,000	10	30	—.14	10	—.64*
$10,000 and above	78	24		33	
Attitude toward intermarriage					
Relatively strict	53	34	—.57*	28	—.10
Relatively lenient	40	13		33	
Number of gentile friends					
No gentile friends	68	25	—.40	38	.14
One or more gentile friends	16	13		31	
Perceived neighborhood racial composition					
Below 75 percent white	13	62	—.75*	15	—.47
75 percent or more white	84	19		33	
Expected racial changes (Proportion of blacks will):					
Decrease or remain same	48	19	.30	38	.31
Increase	50	30		24	
Synagogue membership					
Not a member	7	14	.34	57	.54*
Is a member	91	25		29	
Neighborhood org. part.					
None	41	15	.48*	35	.15
One or more	58	33		28	
Jewish organ. partic.					
None	11	9	—.59*	36	—.14
One or more	86	28		26	

Appendix Table 5C. Continued.

Background characteristics	Sample size	Become more interested		Become less interested	
		% becoming more interested	Q value	% becoming less interested	Q value
Beth Zion organ. partic.					
Low	27	19	.57*	22	.14
High	22	46		27	
Change in attitude toward intermarriage					
Become more lenient or					
remain the same	57	18	.49*	30	.01
Become more strict	34	38		29	
Become more lenient	28	14	.44	29	—.04
Remain same or become					
more strict	63	30		30	
Change in synagogue membership status					
Resign membership or					
remain the same	91	25	—.15	29	—.82*
Become member	5	20		80	
Resign membership	12	17	.28	42	.26
Remain same or become member	84	26		30	
Change in Beth Zion organizational participation					
Become less involved or					
remain the same	33	27	.23	30	.51
Become more involved	16	38		13	
Become less involved	14	36	—.16	29	.15
Remain the same or become					
more involved	35	29		23	
Change in level of Jewish organizational participation					
Become less involved or					
remain the same	61	26	—.07	30	—.13
Become more involved	34	24		35	
Become less involved	29	28	—.09	24	—.25
Remain the same or become					
more involved	66	24		35	

* Q value statistically significant at the .95 confidence level.

Appendix Table 5D. Inter-correlations of independent and dependent variables in regression analysis of determinants of changes in support for synagogue involvement in biracial community activities.

	1	2	3	4	5	6	7	8	9	10	11	12
1		.21	-.09	-.08	-.27	.08	-.26	.08	.18	.15	-.06	.01
2			-.30	-.21	-.27	.16	-.36	-.04	-.04	.14	.16	-.20
3				.28	.09	-.04	.24	.05	.05	.07	-.05	-.07
4					.01	-.06	.51	.10	.21	.12	.11	.04
5						-.46	.23	-.12	-.08	-.01	-.18	.08
6							-.16	.13	.20	.19	.07	-.03
7								.04	.05	.14	-.12	.04
8									.22	.37	-.16	-.45
9										.23	.05	.03
10											-.36	-.09
11												.23
12												

Key: 1. Change in support for inv. in biracial community activities
      2. Age of household head
      3. Educational level
      4. Income
      5. Attitude toward intermarriage
      6. Number of gentile friends

      7. Neighborhood racial composition
      8. Synagogue membership status
      9. Community organizational participation
     10. Jewish organizational participation
     11. Changes in Jewish organizational participation
     12. Changes in synagogue membership status

For definitions of variables, see Tables 2 and 5, Chapter 7.

References

Abrams, Charles, 'The Housing Problem and the Negro', *Daedalus,* 95 No. 1 (Winter 1966), 64-76.

Advisory Committee to the Department of Housing and Urban Development, *Freedom of Choice in Housing: Opportunities and Constraints.* Washington, D.C., National Academy of Sciences, 1972.

Ahlbrandt, Roger S. and Paul C. Brophy, *Neighborhood Revitalization.* Lexington, Mass., Lexington Books, 1975.

Aldrich, Howard, 'Ecological Succession in Racially Changing Neighborhoods: A Review of the Literature', *Urban Affairs Quarterly,* 10 No. 3 (March 1975), 327-48.

Allport, Gordon W., *The Nature of Prejudice.* Boston, Beacon, 1958.

Arthur D. Little Inc., *East Cleveland: Response to Urban Change.* Boston, Arthur D. Little Inc., 1969.

Barresi, Charles M., 'Racial Transition in an Urban Neighborhood', *Growth and Change,* 3 (July 1972), 16-22.

Berelson, Bernard, and Gary Steiner, *Human Behavior: An Inventory of Scientific Findings.* New York, Harcourt, Brace and World, 1964.

Bertsch, Dale F., and Ann M. Shafor, 'A Regional Housing Plan: The Miami Valley Regional Planning Commission Experience', *Planners Notebook,* 1 No. 1 (April 1971).

Berube, Maurice R. and Marilyn Gittel, Eds., *Confrontation at Ocean-Hill Brownsville.* New York, Praeger, 1969.

Beshers, James M., *Urban Social Structure.* New York, Free Press, 1962.

Bigart, Homer, 'U.S. Helps Poor to Rent Own Homes', *New York Times,* July 9, 1972.

Blumer, Herbert, 'Social Science and the Desegregation Process', *Annals of the American Academy of Political and Social Science*, 304 (1956), 137-143.

Bogardus, Emory S., 'A Social Distance Scale', *Sociology and Social Research,* 17 (1933), 265-71.

Bogardus, Emory S., *Immigration and Race Attitudes.* Boston, Heath, 1928.

Bogardus, Emory S., 'Measuring Social Distance', *Journal of Applied Sociology,* 9 (1925), 299-308.

Bradburn, Norman, Seymour Sudman and Galen Gockel, *Side by Side: Integrated Neighborhoods in America.* Chicago, Quadrangle Books, 1971.

Bressler, Marvin, 'The Myers' Case: An Instance of Successful Racial Invasion', *Social Problems,* 8 No. 2 (Fall 1960), 126-42.

Brown, H. James, 'Changes in Workplace and Residential Locations', *Journal of the American Institute of Planners,* 41 No. 1 (January 1975), 32-39.

Brown, W., 'Access to Housing: The Role of the Real Estate Industry', *Economic Geography,* 48 (1972), 66-78.

Bullough, B., *Social Psychological Barriers to Housing Desegregation.* Los Angeles, Graduate School of Business Administration, University of California, 1969.

Burgess, Ernest W., 'Residential Segregation in American Cities', *Annals of the American Academy of Political and Social Science,* 140 (Nov. 1928), 105-115.

Butler, Edgar W., and Edward J. Kaiser, 'Prediction of Residential Movement and Spatial

Allocation', *Urban Affairs Quarterly,* 16, No. 4 (June, 1971), 477-97.

Butler, Edgar W., Georges Sabagh and Maurice D. Van Arsdol, Jr., 'Demographic and Social Psychological Factors in Residential Mobility', *Sociology and Social Research,* 48 (January, 1964), 138-54.

Caplan, Eleanor K. and Eleanor P. Wolf, 'Factors Affecting Racial Change in Two Middle Income Areas', *Phylon,* 21, No. 3 (Fall, 1960) 225-33.

Cerra, Frances, 'Detailed Study Charges Mortgage Bias by Major Savings Banks in Brooklyn', *New York Times,* December 6, 1976.

Chambers, Marcia, 'Brooklyn Synagogue to Hear Sound of Shofar Last Time', *New York Times,* October, 1976.

Cohen, Oscar, 'The Case for Benign Quotas', *Phylon,* 21, No. 1 (Spring, 1960), 20-29.

Coleman, James S., 'Population Stability and Equal Rights', *Society,* 14, No. 4 (May/June 1977), 34-36.

Coleman, James S., Sara D. Kelly and John A. Moore, *Trends in School Segregation, 1968-73.* Washington, D.C., Urban Institute, 1973.

Connolly, H., 'Black Movement into the Suburbs', *Urban Affairs Quarterly,* 9, No. 1 (September, 1973), 91-111.

Council of Jewish Federations and Welfare Funds, *Winners 1974: William J. Shroder Awards.* New York, Council of Jewish Federations and Welfare Funds, 1974.

Cuomo, Mario Matthew, *Forest Hills Diary.* New York, Random House, 1974.

Delaney, Paul, 'Black Middle Class Joining the Exodus to White Suburbia', *New York Times,* January 4, 1976a.

Delaney, Paul, 'Dayton Suburbs Tackle Problems of "Fair Share" Housing', *New York Times,* November 17, 1974.

Delaney, Paul, 'Suburbs Fighting Back as Crime Rises', *New York Times,* August 30, 1976b.

Dionne, E.J., Jr., 'What New Yorkers Think of City: Blacks are the Least Pessimistic', *New York Times,* August 28, 1977.

Dobriner, William M., *Class in Suburbia.* Englewood Cliffs, N.J., Prentice-Hall, 1963.

Downs, Anthony, 'Alternative Futures for the American Ghetto', *Daedalus,* 97, No. 4 (Fall, 1968), 1331-79.

Downs, Anthony, 'An Economic Analysis of Property Values and Race', *Housing Urban America.* Edited by Jon Pynoos, *et al,* Chicago, Aldine, 1973, 267-73.

Droettboom, Theodore, Jr., Ronald J. McAllister, Edward J. Kaiser and Edgar W. Butler, 'Urban Violence and Residential Mobility', *Journal of the American Institute of Planners,* 37 (September, 1971), 319-25.

Duncan, Otis Dudley, and Beverly Duncan, *The Negro Population of Chicago: A Study of Residential Succession.* Chicago, University of Chicago Press, 1957.

Farley, Reynolds, 'Integrating Residential Neighborhoods', *Society,* 14, No. 4 (May/June, 1977), 38-40.

Farley, Reynolds, 'Racial Integration in the Public Schools, 1967 to 1972', *Sociological Focus,* 8 (January 1975), 3-26.

Farrell, William E., 'The Hyde Park – Kenwood Section of Chicago: An Integrated Inner City Neighborhood that Works', *New York Times,* April 27, 1973.

Farrell, William E., 'Redlining, Whether Cause or Effect, is No Help', *New York Times,* September 14, 1975.

Fauman, S. Joseph, 'Housing Discrimination, Changing Neighborhoods and Public Schools', *Journal of Social Issues,* 13, No. 4 (1957), 21-30.

Ferretti, Fred, 'After 70 Years South Bronx Street is at Dead End', *New York Times,* October 21, 1977.

Fiske, Edward B., 'Scholar Eases Criticism of Study of White Flight', *New York Times,* September 2, 1977.

Foley, Donald L., 'Institutional and Contextual Factors Affecting the Housing Choices of Minority Residents', *Segregation in Residential Areas.* Edited by Amos H. Hawley and Vincent P. Rock. Washington, D.C., National Academy of Sciences, 1973, 85-147.

Ford Foundation Letter, 'Open Housing: Slow Progress', October 1, 1976.

Fowler, Glenn, 'Preservation of Little Italy Urged', *New York Times,* September 3, 1976.

Fowler, Glenn, 'State Drafts Program to Increase Mortgage Lending in Inner Cities', *New York Times,* May 11, 1977.

Freeman, Linton C. and Morris H. Sunshine, *Patterns of Residential Segregation.* Cambridge, Mass., Schenkman Publishing, 1970.

Fried, Joseph P., 'The Assaults on Zoning in Fortress Suburbia', *New York Times,* April 13, 1977.

Fried, Joseph P., 'Housing Abandonment Spreads in Bronx and Parts of Brooklyn', *New York Times,* April 12, 1976a.

Fried, Joseph P., 'Soliciting of Real Estate is Banned in Two Boroughs', *New York Times,* July 22, 1976b.

Fried, Marc, 'Grieving for a Lost Home', *The Urban Condition.* Edited by Leonard Duhl. New York, Basic Books, 1963, 151-71.

Friedman, Murray, 'Blacks and Jews', *Friday Forum – A Supplement to the Jewish Exponent,* No. 31, December 27, 1974.

Friedman, Murray (Ed), *Overcoming Middle Class Rage.* Philadelphia, Westminster Press, 1971.

Gans, Herbert J., 'The Balanced Community', *Journal of the American Institute of Planners,* 27, No. 3 (August 1961), 176-184.

Gans, Herbert J., *The Urban Villagers.* New York, The Free Press, 1962.

Gettys, Warner E., 'Human Ecology and Social Theory', *Studies in Human Ecology.* Edited by George A. Theodorson. Evanston, Ill., Row Peterson and Company, 1966, 98-103.

Ginsberg, Yona, *Jews in a Changing Neighborhood: The Study of Mattapan.* New York, The Free Press, 1975.

Glantz, Frederick B. and Nancy Delaney, 'Changes in Non-White Residential Patterns in Large Metropolitan Areas, 1960 and 1970', *New England Economic Review,* (March/April 1973), 3-13.

Gordon, Albert I., *Jews in Suburbia.* Boston, Beacon Hill Press, 1959.

Greeley, Andrew M., ' "We" and "They": The Differences Linger', in *Overcoming Middle Class Rage.* Edited by Murray Friedman. Philadelphia, Westminster Press, 1971, 257-268.

Greenleigh Associates, *A Plan to Reduce Prejudice and Discrimination in the Greater Milwaukee Area.* New York, Greenleigh Associates, 1967.

Grier, George and Eunice Grier, 'Equality and Beyond: Housing Segregation in the Great Society', *Daedalus,* 95, No. 1 (Winter 1966), 77-106.

Grodzins, Morton, 'Metropolitan Segregation', *Scientific American,* 197 (October, 1957), 33-41.

Gross, David, 'Mt. Airy Jewish Community Undergoing Change, Exodus', *Jewish Exponent,* March 20, 1973.

Guttentag, Jack M., 'Racial Integration and Home Prices', *Wharton Quarterly,* 4 (Spring 1970).

Hawley, Amos, *Human Ecology: A Theory of Community Structure.* New York, Ronald Press, 1950.

Hershey, Robert D., Jr., 'Working Class in London Resists Incursion by the Gentry', *New York Times,* September 22, 1977.

Hodgart, R.L., *The Process of Expansion of the Negro Ghetto in the Cities of the Northern United States: A Case Study of Cleveland Ohio,* unpublished M. Sc. thesis, Department of Geography, Pennsylvania State University, 1968.

Holsendolph, Ernest, 'Neighborhoods Unite to Help Themselves', *New York Times,* July 6, 1976.

Holsendolph, Ernest, 'Rights Panel Urges New Drive to Build Housing for the Poor', *New York Times,* December 11, 1975.

Hoyt, Homer, *The Structure and Growth of Neighborhoods in American Cities.* Washington, D.C., Federal Housing Administration, 1939.

Isard, Walter, *Methods of Regional Analysis.* New York, John Wiley, 1960.

Janson, Donald, 'Racial Change Slashes Values and Produces Bargains', *New York Times,* January 21, 1973 (Real Estate Section).

Jewish Community Relations Council of Greater Philadelphia, *Survey of Racial Changes in the Wynnefield Area of Philadelphia.* Philadelphia, undated.

Jewish Exponent, 'JCRC Asks HUD to End Redlining', August 6, 1976.

Jewish Exponent, 'New Program Meets Needs in Wynnefield', December 22, 1972.

Johnson, George E., 'Synagogue Survival Strategies in a Rootless Society: A Case Study', *Analysis*, No. 5 (April 15, 1974).

Kadushin, Charles, 'Reason Analysis', *International Encyclopedia of the Social Sciences,* 13 (1968), 338-43.

Kain, John F., *Theories of Residential Location and Realities of Race.* Harvard University Program in Regional Urban Economics, Discussion Paper 47. Cambridge, Harvard University, 1970.

Kandell, Jonathan, 'Jewish Group Buying Homes in Crown Heights to Stabilize the Community', *New York Times,* January 9, 1972.

Kifner, John, 'Bushwick Struggles Not to Become South Bronx', *New York Times,* October 24, 1977.

King, Wayne, 'District Integration Pressed in Atlanta',*New York Times,* November 16, 1977.

Klausner, Samuel Z. and David P. Varady,*Synagogues Without Ghettos.* Philadelphia, Center for Research on the Acts of Man, 1970.

Kneeland, Douglas E., 'An Ethnic Chicago Neighborhood Tries to Explain its Racial Problems', *New York Times*, August 7, 1977.

Labovitz, Sherman. *Attitudes Toward Blacks Among Jews: Historical Antecedents and Current Concerns.* Saratoga, California, R and E Research Associates, 1975.

Land, Kenneth C., 'Principles of Path Analysis', *Sociological Methodology – 1969.* Edited by Edgar F. Borgatta. San Francisco, Jossey Bass Inc., 1969, 3-37.

Laurenti, Luigi, *Property Values and Race: Studies in Seven Cities.* Berkeley, University of California Press, 1960.

Lee, Trevor R., *Race and Residence.* Oxford, Oxford University Press, 1977.

Lichtenstein, Grace, ' "Transitional" Crown Heights Now in Midst of Comeback',*New York Times,* August 1, 1974.

Lindsey, Robert, 'Los Angeles Schools Plan Busing Amid White Flight', *New York Times,* October 11, 1977.

Long, Norton E., 'A Marshall Plan for Cities', *The Public Interest,* No. 46 (Winter, 1977) 48-58.

Lyndon, Christopher, 'Carter Defends All-White Areas', *New York Times,* April 7, 1976.

McEntire, Davis, *Residence and Race*. Berkeley, University of California Press, 1960.

McFadden, Robert D., 'White Youths Terrorize Black Family in Staten Island Home', *New York Times,* August 16, 1976.

McFall, Trudy, 'Fair Share Housing: The Twin Cities Story', *Planning,* 43, No. 7 (August, 1977), 22-25.

Manley, Robert E., 'School Desegregation in the North: A Post Milliken Strategy for Obtaining Metropolitan Relief', *Saint Louis University Law Journal,* 20, No. 4 (1976) 585-609.

Marcus, Jacob Rader, 'Background for the History of American Jewry', *The American Jew: A Reappraisal.* Edited by Oscar I. Janowsky. Philadelphia, Jewish Publication Society, 1964, 1-26.

Mayer, Albert J., 'Change Without Conflict: A Case Study of Neighborhood Racial Change in Detroit', *Studies in Housing and Minority Groups.* Edited by Nathan Glazer and Davis McEntire. Berkeley, University of California Press, 1960, 298-320.

Millen, James S., 'Factors Affecting Racial Mixing in Residential Areas', *Segregation in Residential Areas.* Edited by Amos H. Hawley and Vincent P. Rock. Washington, D.C., National Academy of Sciences, 1973, 148-71.

Molotch, Harvey L., *Managed Integration: Dilemmas of Doing Good in the City.* Berkeley, California, University of California Press, 1972.

Moore, Eric G., *Residential Mobility in the City.* A. A. G. Resource Paper No. 13. Washington, D.C., Commission on College Geography, 1972.

Moran, Nancy, 'New Yorkers Find Familiar Ills in Mt. Vernon', *New York Times,* October 24, 1969.

Morrill, Richard I., 'The Negro Ghetto: Problems and Alternatives', *Geographical Review,* 55 (July, 1965), 339-361.

New York Times, 'Court Insists Intent Be Shown As Test of Bias,' January 16, 1977.

New York Times, 'Surinamese Add to Woes of Dutch', October 1, 1974.

Northwood, Lawrence K. and Ernest A. T. Barth, *Urban Desegregation: Negro Pioneers and Their White Neighbors.* Seattle, University of Washington Press, 1965.

Northwood, Lawrence K. and Louise H. Klein, 'The Tipping Point – A Questionable Quality of Neighborhoods', *Journal of Intergroup Relations,* 4 No. 4 (Autumn 1965), 226-39.

Oelsner, Lesley, 'Justices Upset Ban on House Sale Signs', *New York Times,* May 3, 1977.

Øyen, Ørjar, *Ecological Context and Residential Differentiation.* Oslo, Universitetstorlaget, 1964.

Park, Robert, 'Human Ecology', *American Journal of Sociology,* 42 (July, 1936), 1-15.

Park, Robert, 'Succession: An Ecological Concept', *American Sociological Review,* 1 (April, 1936), 171-79.

Peach, Ceri (Ed.), *Urban Social Segregation.* London and New York, Longman and Company, 1975.

Pettigrew, Thomas, 'Attitudes on Race and Housing: A Social Psychological View', in *Segregation in Residential Areas.* Edited by A. Hawley and V. Rock. Washington, D.C., National Academy of Sciences, 1973, 21-84.

Philadelphia City Planning Commission, *Housing Characteristics: 1960 and 1970 Philadelphia Census Tracts.* Philadelphia, Philadelphia City Planning Commission, undated.

Pickvance, C. G., 'Life Cycle, Housing Tenure and Intra-Urban Residential Mobility: A Causal Model', *Sociological Review* (new series), 21, No. 2 (May 1973), 279-97.

Rabinovitz, Francine F. and William J. Siembieda, *Minorities in Suburbs: The Los Angeles Experience.* Lexington, Mass., Lexington Books, 1977.

Rapkin, Chester and William Grigsby, *The Demand for Housing in Racially Mixed Areas*. Berkeley, University of California Press, 1960.

Ravitz, Mel J., 'Effects of Urban Renewal on Community Racial Patterns', *Journal of Social Issues*, 13 No. 4, 1957, 38-49.

Reed, Roy, 'British Ponder Ban on Violence Prone Carnival', *New York Times*, August 31, 1977b.

Reed, Roy, 'Carnival in London Ends Amid Violence', *New York Times*, August 30, 1977a.

Reinhold, Robert, 'A Priest is Stirring the Melting Pot to Revitalize Ethnic Neighborhoods', *New York Times*, April 20, 1977a.

Reinhold, Robert, 'Middle Class Return Displaces Some Urban Poor', *New York Times*, June 5, 1977b.

Roistacher, Elizabeth, 'Residential Mobility: Planners, Movers and Multiple Movers', *Five Thousand American Families: Patterns of Economic Progress*, Volume 3. Edited by Greg J. Duncan and James N. Morgan. Ann Arbor, Survey Research Center, 1975, 79-106.

Rose, Harold M., 'The Development of An Urban Subsystem: The Case of the Negro Ghetto', *Annals of the Association of American Geographers*, 60, No. 1 (March, 1970), 1-17.

Rose, Harold M., *Social Processes in The City: Race and Urban Residential Choice*. Resource Paper No. 6. Commission on College Geography. Washington, D.C., Association of American Geographers, 1969.

Rossi, Peter H., *Why Families Move*. Glencoe, Illinois, Free Press, 1955.

Sabagh, Georges, Maurice Van Arsdol, Jr., and Edgar Butler, 'Some Determinants of Intra-metropolitan Mobility: Conceptual Considerations', *Social Forces*, 48 (September 1969), 89-98.

Selznick, Gertrude J. and Stephen Steinberg, *The Tenacity of Prejudice*. New York, Harper and Row, 1969.

Sherif, Muzafer and Carolyn Sherif, *Groups in Harmony and Tension*. New York, Harper, 1953.

Simmons, James W., 'Changing Residences in the City: A Review of Intraurban Mobility', *Geographical Review*, 58 (October, 1968), 622-51.

Sklare, Marshall, *America's Jews*. New York, Random House, 1971.

Sklare, Marshall, 'Jews, Ethnics and the American City', *Commentary*, 53, No. 4 (April, 1972), 70-77.

Sobel, B.Z. and Mae Sobel, 'Negroes and Jews: Minority Groups in Conflict', *Judaism* 15 (Winter, 1966), 3-22.

Sternlieb, George, Robert W. Burchell, James A. Hughes and Franklin J. James, 'Housing Abandonment in the Urban Core', *Journal of the American Institute of Planners*, 40, No. 5 (September, 1974), 321-32.

Stevens, William K., 'Hamtramck Strives to Retain its Polish Character', *New York Times*, October, 1974.

Sullivan, Ronald, 'Sales of Homes By Race Alleged in a Bergen Suit', *New York Times*, March 8, 1976.

Taeuber, Karl and Alma Taeuber, *Negroes in Cities: Residential Segregation and Neighborhood Change*. Chicago, Aldine, 1965.

Thomas, Wesley and William Simon, *Migration and Racial Change in Bond Hill and Kennedy Heights*. Cincinnati, Department of Urban Development, City of Cincinnati, 1976.

Thompson, Wilbur R., *A Preface to Urban Economics*. Baltimore, Johns Hopkins Press, 1965 (1968).

Tobin, Gary, 'Why Do People Move?', *Focus-Midwest*, 11, No. 73, (undated) 10-14.

United States Department of Housing and Urban Development, *Abandoned Housing Research: A Compendium.* Washington, D.C., U.S. Government Printing Office, 1973.

Van Arsdol, Maurice D., Jr., Georges Sabagh and Edgar W. Butler, 'Retrospective and Subsequent Metropolitan Residential Mobility', *Demography,* 5, No. 1 (1968), 249-67.

Varady, David P., 'Determinants of Mobility in an Inner City Community', *Regional Science Perspectives,* 5 (1975), 154-178.

Varady, David P., 'The Ethnic Factor and Moving Decisions in a Racially Changing Community', *Regional Science Perspectives,* 7, No. 2 (1977), 135-164.

Varady, David P., *The Household Migration Decision in Racially Changing Neighborhoods.* Philadelphia, Penna., University of Pennsylvania Doctoral Dissertation, 1971.

Varady, David P., 'The Mobility Process in a Racially Changing Community', *Regional Science Perspectives,* 8 (1978) forthcoming.

Varady, David P., 'Moving Intentions and Behavior in the Cincinnati Model Neighborhood', *Bulletin of the Association of the American Collegiate Schools of Planning,* 12, No. 1 (Spring, 1974), 1-3.

Varady, David P., 'White Moving Plans in a Racially Changing Middle Class Community', *Journal of the American Institute of Planners,* 40, No. 5 (September, 1974), 360-70.

Waldron, Martin, 'Arson Blamed in Fire at Home of Black Family in Rosedale', *New York Times,* September 6, 1975.

Westie, Frank R., 'Negro White Status Differentials and Social Distance', *American Sociological Review,* 11, No. 5 (October 1952), 550-58.

Wilkes, Paul, 'As the Blacks Move In, the Ethnics Move Out', *New York Times Magazine,* January 24, 1971.

Williams, Dennis and Pamela Ellis Simons, 'Integration: Success in Oak Park', *Newsweek,* October 17, 1977.

Wirth, Louis, *The Ghetto.* Chicago, University of Chicago Press, 1928 (1956).

Wolf, Eleanor P., 'The Baxter Area, 1960-1962: A New Trend in Neighborhood Change', *Phylon,* 26 (Winter, 1965), 344-353.

Wolf, Eleanor P., 'The Invasion Succession Sequence As a Self-Fulfilling Prophecy', *Journal of Social Issues,* 13, No. 4 (1957), 7-20.

Wolf, Eleanor P., 'The Tipping Point in Racially Changing Neighborhoods', *Journal of the American Institute of Planners,* 29 (August, 1963), 217-22.

Wolf, Eleanor P. and Charles N. Lebeaux with Shirley Terreberry and Helen Saperstein, *Change and Renewal in An Urban Community: Five Case Studies of Detroit.* New York, Praeger, 1969.

Wolf, Eleanor P. and Charles N. Lebeaux, 'Class and Race in the Changing City', *Urban Research and Policy Planning.* Edited by Leo F. Schnore and Henry Fagin. Beverly Hills, Sage Publications, 1967.

Wolpert, Julian, 'Behavioral Aspects of the Decision to Migrate', *Papers of the Regional Science Association,* 15 (1965), 159-69.

Wooten, James T., 'Busing May Change the Philadelphia Story', *New York Times,* August 3, 1975.

Yarmolinsky, Adam, 'Reassuring the Small Homeowner', *The Public Interest,* 22 (Winter, 1971), 106-110.

Zehner, Robert B. and F. Stuart Chapin, Jr., *Across The City Line: A White Community in Transition.* Lexington, Massachusetts, Lexington Books, 1974.

Index

Abandonment, housing, 4, 28
Abrams, Charles, 29
Accessibility to work, *see* Commuting
Age, 16, 26, 28, 40, 48-49, 50, 52-54, 56,
    63, 65, 71, 80, 98, 99, 108, 122, 123,
    129, 139
Aggregative principle, 32
Allport, Gordon W., 34
Amsterdam, 7
    Bijlmermeer, 7
    Gliphove, 7
Apartments, high rise, 65, 80, 112-113,
    116
Arthur D. Little Inc., 2, 5, 6, 15
Armor, David, 28
Assimilation, 14, 18, 19
Automobile driving, 18, 81, 84, 91, 98,
    111

Baroni, Geno, 142
Barresi, Charles M., 21
Barth, Ernest A. T., 20
Belfast, Northern Ireland, 6
Berelson, Bernard, 34
Bertsch, Dale, 138n.
Berube, Maurice R., 121
Beth Zion organizational participation,
    122, 123, 125
Biracial community action, 122-123,
    128-133, 141
Blacks
    alienation, 2, 7
    attitudes toward racial change, 1n.
    black housing market, 22, 29, 46, 64,
    78
    black-Jewish relations, 18, 64,
    120-133, 140-142
    black-white differences, 16, 25-26,
    27, 28, 30-31, 36, 48-56, 65
    black-white social contacts, 1-2, 65,
    66, 88n., 112
    distinct cultural group, as a, 27, 35,
    40-42

    ghettos, 2, 7, 15, 16, 21, 24, 26, 27,
    28, 29, 30, 35, 40-42, 58, 63-64,
    136-139
    housing demand, 15, 16, 21, 22, 24,
    29, 30, 64, 136-139
    housing search behavior, 15, 16, 26,
    40n.
    inter-ethnic group tensions, 4
    middle class, 1n., 2n., 20, 24, 25, 26,
    29, 52
    militants, 121
    mobility related attitudes, 16, 20
    stabilization programs, attitude
    toward, 24; *see also* Stabilization
    Programs
    stereotypes of, 23-24, 36, 88n.
    suburbanization, 2-3, 7, 22, 23
    white reactions to, 15, 20-21, 34, 64,
    141-142
Block clubs, 24, 45, 136
Blockbusting, 20-21
Bogardus, Emory S., 86-87
Boston, Mattapan community, 3-4, 18, 30,
    61, 104
Bradburn, Norman, 17, 30, 34, 35
Brown, H. James, 99
Brown, W., 36
Burgess, Ernest W., 14
Busing, 27-28
Butler, Edgar W., 85

Caplan, Eleanor K., 22-23, 70
CAT test, 58
Catholics, 39, 46, 79
Carter, Jimmy, 141n.
Census, federal, 26, 52, 58, 59, 61, 68
Chapin, F. Stuart, 2, 17
Chicago, 14
    Arlington Heights, 136n., 137n.
    Englewood Park, 4
    Hyde Park-Kenwood, 21
    Marquette, 4
    Oak Park, 21

South Shore, 21, 26, 30, 61
West Side, 14
Children, 27, 48, 51, 69, 78-79, 83, 98
Chinese, 142n.
Churches, 3, 4, 18, 30, 39, 138-142
Civic Associations, *see* Resident
Associations
Civil rights movement, 120-121
Cleveland
Cleveland Heights, 21, 24-25
East Cleveland, 2, 5, 30, 31
Ludlow, 21, 22
Coleman, James, 27-28
Commercial areas, *see* Shopping
Community development corporations,
125, 128
Community standards, 5, 25, 26-31, 40,
43, 56-63, 64-65, 104, 140-141
See also Crime, Housing, Property
values, Schools, Shopping
Commuting, 92, 99, 114
Consumer Price Index, 53
Crime, 30-31, 32, 45, 61-63, 65, 104,
107-108, 111, 118, 135, 140
Cuomo, Mario M., 121

Dayton, Ohio, 138
Delaney, Nancy, 2
Demarest, New Jersey, 137n.
Density, household, 59
Detached homes, 61, 70, 78, 83, 97-98,
101, 135
Detroit, 98n., 138, 142
Baxter, 18-19
Hamtramck, 142
Russel Woods, 22, 34
Discrimination, 7, 34, 39, 88n., 95-96, 136
Dispersal policies, 136-139, 142
Dobriner, William M., 36
Downs, Anthony, 27, 29n., 35, 138
Droettboom, Theodore Jr., 31
Duncan, Otis Dudley and Beverly, 1,
14-15, 26

Ecology
concepts, 1, 14
criticisms of, 31-32
ecological consequences of racial
transition, 25-31, 48-63
Education, 6, 18, 25, 26, 49, 51, 52-53,
65, 68-69, 73, 78, 83, 122, 123, 129,
139
Ethnicity

ethnic change, 1, 6, 14, 39, 142n.; *see
also* Blacks, Jews, Racial Transition
Process, Whites
ethnic communities, 1, 3, 4, 84,
141-142
ethnic factors and mobility, 16,
17-20, 84, 101, 119, 135; *see also*
Jews-religious characteristics and
mobility
ethnic groups, *see* Blacks, Jews,
Italians, etc.
ethnic movement, 142
ethnic organizations, 138-139
inter-ethnic group tensions, 4
Euphemisms, 45n.

Fair share concept, 138
Family size, 48, 49
Family structure, 49, 52, 63-64
Farley, Reynolds, 28
Financial resources, *see* Income
Foley, Donald L., 16
For sale signs, 5
Foreign immigration, 1, 7, 14
Freeman, Linton C., 16-17
Fried, Marc, 3
Friedman, Murray, 4, 20, 121
Friendships, 4, 36, 65, 70, 90, 97

Gangs, 59, 61, 135
Gans, Herbert, 19, 36
Gentile friends, 122, 123
Gentrification, 36
Germans, 4, 5, 14
Ghettos
black, 2, 7, 15, 16, 21, 22, 24, 26, 27,
28, 29, 30, 31, 34, 40-42, 58, 63, 64
136-139; *see also* Blacks
foreign examples, 6-7
ghetto dispersal versus enrichment
strategy, 138
Jewish, 4, 39; *see also* Jews
Polish, 20; *see also* Poles
Ginsberg, Yona, 4, 15, 18, 21, 24, 30, 61,
104
Glantz, Frederick B., 2
Gordon, Albert I., 31
Governmental services, *see* Public services
Great Britain, 7
Greeks, 6, 14
Greeley, Andrew, 20
Greenleigh Associates, 5
Grier, George and Eunice, 3

Grigsby, William, 6n., 22, 55
Grodzins, Morton, 21
Guttentag, Jack M., 30
Guttman scales, 88n., 91, 125

Hawley, Amos, 14
Homeownership, 20, 26, 29, 49, 51,
    54-56, 65, 71-72, 80, 99
Housing
    conservation programs, 5
    housing quality and mobility, 14, 16,
    17n., 20, 23, 40, 46, 48, 63, 69-70,
    78, 97-98, 101, 107, 110-111, 118,
    135, 139
    impact of racial change on quality,
    4-5, 7, 28-29, 58-60, 104
    opportunities, low and moderate
    income, 16, 64, 136-137
    rehabilitation, 36
    see also Metropolitan housing policies
Housing search
    actual selection of a new location,
    115-116
    criteria utilized, 104, 109
    geographic scope, 105, 112-114, 118
    number of communities considered,
    114-115, 118
    time involved, 104-105, 114-115, 118
    types of areas considered, 135
Hoyt, Homer, 14

Income, 25-26, 28, 36-37, 49, 51-54, 65,
    72, 89, 97, 99, 104, 122, 123, 129
Integrated communities, stable
    defined, 22
    features desired by whites, 100,
    134-135
    incidence, 6, 22
    obstacles in attaining, 65, 140; see
    also Proximity to ghetto, Crime
Integration attitudes, see Racial Prejudice
Intermarriage, 81, 84, 90-91, 101, 105,
    109, 112, 113-114, 118-119, 122,
    123, 128, 132, 135, 141
Invasion and succession, 1, 14
Irish, 4, 14
Italians, 4, 6, 14, 19-20, 63-64

Jews
    assimilation, 18, 19
    black-Jewish relations, 18, 64,
    120-133, 140-142
    family structure, 18, 39-40, 63-64
    impacts of racial change, 3-4, 90

    Jewish organizational participation,
    122, 123, 125, 128
    Lubavitch Hasidic sect, 19
    Orthodox, 18, 19, 70-71, 81, 83, 91,
    98, 101, 111
    philanthropism, 24
    religious characteristics and mobility,
    18, 37, 67, 70-71, 79, 81, 83, 89-91,
    98, 101, 105, 111, 118-119, 135, 141
    socio-economic mobility, 63
    stabilization programs, 19, 24-25, 64,
    120-133, 135-142
    voting patterns, 121
    vulnerability to racial change, 3-4, 6,
    14, 16, 17-19, 23, 27, 31, 39-40,
    63-64, 70, 98n.
    see also Ethnicity, Religious Changes,
    Synagogues, Wynnefield-history
Jewish Community Relations Councils, 24
    Philadelphia, 43, 45-46, 48, 64, 139
Jewish Federations, 24
    Boston, 64
    Cleveland, 24-25
    Philadelphia, 45, 61, 64
Job transfers, 72, 80, 99
Johnson, George, 18

Kadushin, Charles, 32, 102
Klein, Louise H., 21
King, Rev. Martin Luther, Jr., 4

Labovitz, Sherman, 121n.
Land, Kenneth C., 93n.
Land ownership, 4
Landlord-tenant relationship, 28-29
Latent causal relationships, 32-33
Laurenti, Luigi, 29
Law of Dominance, 35
Lebeaux, Charles N., 27
Lee, Trevor, 7
Length of residence, 72, 80, 99
Life cycle position, 51, 55, 71; see also
    Age, Children, Family size, etc.
Life styles, 65, 70, 79, 80, 83, 90, 97
Likert scale, 125
Linearity assumption, 93n.
Lithuanians, 4, 14
Little Italy Restoration Association, 142n.
London, 7
    Islington, 36
    Notting Hill, 7
Long, Norton, 19
Los Angeles, 2, 28

Pasadena, 2
Watts, 2
Louisville, Kentucky, 138
Lower Merion Township
   accessibility to downtown
      Philadelphia, 8-9
   crime, 61-63, 107-108, 111
   history, 39
   housing conditions, 8-9, 104, 107,
      110-111, 118
   housing density, 8
   housing search, 109-119
   location, 8-10
   population size, 10
   potential mobility rate, 73
   property values, 61
   reasons for moving, 105-109,
      118-119
Lubavitch Hasidic sect, 19

McFall, Trudy, 138
Mailed questionnaires, 8, 103, 144-146,
   148-150
Maltese, 6
Manifest causal relationships, 32
Master plans, 23, 45, 136
Mattapan Organization, Boston, 24, 64
Mayer, Albert J., 34
Melting pot, 142
Metropolitan housing policies, 136-139,
   142
Metropolitan school districts, 136-139
Milwaukee, 5
Minneapolis-St. Paul, 138
Mobility
   factors influencing, 68-69, 81-101,
      134-135, 139
   forced movers, 104
   how measured, 86
   impact on housing conservation
      programs, 5
   models, 31-33, 85
   moving desires, and, 85
   moving plans, and, 68n., 85, 86,
      99-100, 134
   process, as a, 32, 102-118, 134, 135,
      140
   see also Tipping point, Whites - panic
      moves
Molotch, Harvey L., 15, 21, 22, 24, 26,
   27, 30, 45n., 61
Moore, Eric G., 32, 71-72, 99, 104

Morrill, Richard I., 16
Mortgage loans, 19, 25, 29, 139
Mt. Laurel Township, New Jersey, 137n.
Moving plans
   factors affecting, 67-83, 134-135,
      139-140
   how measured, 67-68
   mobility behavior, and, 68n., 85, 86,
      99-100, 134
Multicollinearity, 93n.
Multiple earners, 25
Neighborhood organizations, 70, 79-80,
   83, 90, 97, 122, 123, 128, 130-131
Neighborhood quality, see Community
   standards
Neighborhood racial composition, 34-35,
   68, 73, 83, 84, 88, 96, 100, 122-123,
   129, 130-131, 134
Netherlands, 7
New York City, 1n., 121
   Bronx Park South, 5
   Brooklyn, 5-6
   Brooklyn Heights, 1
   Brownsville, 18, 121
   Bushwick, 4, 19
   Crown Heights, 19
   East Flatbush, 3
   Forest Hills, 121
   Levittown, 36
   Little Italy, 142
   Mt. Vernon, 3
   Park Slope, 1
   Queens, 5-6
   South Bronx, 4-5
New York City Planning Commission,
   142n.
New York State, 29
Northwood, Lawrence K., 20, 21
Notting Hill Carnival, London, 7

Ocean Hill-Brownsville teachers dispute
   Brooklyn, New York, 121
Occupations, 25, 51, 53-54, 65, 89
Oslo, Norway, 89
Øyen, Øryar, 89

Park, Robert, 14
Path diagrams, 93, 96
Peach, Ceri, 6
Pettigrew, Thomas, 36
Philadelphia, 22, 78, 79
   Northeast Philadelphia, 114

Queens Village, 1
Society Hill, 1
South Philadelphia, 39
West Mt. Airy, 3, 21, 30
West Philadelphia, 40, 56, 63, 78
see also Lower Merion, Wynnefield
Philadelphia Board of Education, 58
Philadelphia Office of Finance, 58n.
Planners, 7, 45, 140
Poles, 4, 14, 20, 142
Police, 6, 140; *see also* Crime

Prejudice, *see* Racial Prejudice
Property values, 29-30, 61, 78, 80, 113
Proximity to ghetto, 16, 21, 23, 63
Public services, 5-6, 23, 36, 45, 136
Push and pull factors, 14-20

Quality of life, *see* Community standards
Quotas, benign, 22

Rabinovitz, Francine F., 2-3
Race related attitudes, 84; *see also*
    Racial prejudice, Neighborhood racial
    composition, etc.
Racial changes, expected, 35-36, 84,
    88-89, 97, 104, 122, 123, 128, 136,
    142
Racial conflict, *see* Violence, Whites -
    reactions to black inmigration
Racial prejudice
    components, 88n.
    defined, 33, 69n, 86-88
    discriminatory behavior, and, 34,
        95-96
    factors affecting, 6, 69, 78
    mobility behavior, and, 34, 68-69, 84,
        86-88, 93, 95-96, 100, 134-135
    neighborhood vulnerability to change,
        and, 16-17
    rates of transition, and, 22
Racial residential segregation, 6
Racial transition process
    impact on societal problems, 1-6
    rates of transition, 21, 22-23, 26-27,
        40, 45, 46, 48, 56, 58, 70, 136
    whites replacing blacks, 1
    see also: Blacks, Churches, Crime,
    Ethnicity, Housing, Jews, Property
    values, Push-pull factors, Real estate
    brokers, Resident associations,
    Schools, Synagogues, Tipping point,
    Violence, Whites

Racism, 4
Rapkin, Chester, 6n., 22, 55
Rates of racial change, *see* Racial
    transition process
Real estate brokers, 5, 16, 20-21, 22, 23,
    45, 46, 136
Reason analysis, 102, 118
Reasons for moving, 103-109, 118-119,
    134-135, 140
Redevelopment areas, 22
Redlining, 29, 139
Reference group theory, 89
Relatives, 90, 92n., 93n., 97
Religious changes, 38-39, 46, 47, 89, 97
Religious characterics, *see* Jews
Resident associations, 5, 23-24, 34, 45-46,
    65-66, 120, 129-133 *passim,*
    135-136, 138-139
Resorgimiento, 142n
Richmond, Virginia, 138
Riots, 2, 121
Roistacher, Elizabeth, 99
Rose, Harold M., 15
Rossi, Peter H., 102
Row houses, 39, 63, 78, 135

Sabagh, Georges, 70
St. Louis
    Italian Hill, 19
    University City, 6, 17n., 18n., 21,
        27
Schools
    private and parochial, 18, 27, 56, 58,
        79
    public, 2, 3, 26-28, 32, 36, 43, 56-59,
        65, 69, 79, 104, 107, 109-110,
        123-124, 133, 142
    see also Metropolitan school districts
Security patrols, 45, 140; *see also* Crime
Segregation
    schools, *de facto,* 2
    residential, 1, 2
Selznick, Gertrude J., 88n.
Shafor, Ann, 138n.
Sherif, Muzafer and Carolyn, 89
Shopping, 4, 30, 61, 90, 97, 107
Siembieda, William J., 2
Simmons, James W., 17, 84
Sklare, Marshall, 18, 24
Social class
    difficulties in maintaining mixture, 36
    expected changes in, 36

Social distance scales, 86, 87
Social mobility, 14, 15, 18, 52, 63
Social patterns and contacts, 116; *see also*
    Friendships, Relatives
Socio-economic characteristics
    racial transition rates, and, 22
    shifts accompanying racial change,
    25-26, 52-56, 64-65
    see also Education, Income,
    Occupation
South Shore Commission, Chicago, 24,
    45n.
Stabilization programs
    Jewish communities, 19, 24-25, 64,
    120-133, 135-142
    localistic programs, 5, 6, 15, 19, 25,
    29, 43-45, 64, 138-140
    metropolitan-wide housing and
    educational policies, 136-139, 142
    suburban areas, 17n.
    synagogues, 24, 120-133, 140-142
Steering, racial, 21
Steinberg, Stephen, 88n.
Steiner, Gary, 34
Stereotypes, racial, 23-24, 36, 88n.
Suburbs
    blacks in, 2-3, 7, 22, 23
    crime, 31, 107
    housing opportunities, 16, 64,
    136-137
    movement to, 25
    no-growth philosophy, 136
    property values, 69
    stabilization programs, 17n.
    way of life, as a, 18
Sunshine, Morris H., 16-17
Surinamese, 7
Synagogues
    affiliation, reasons for, 81
    allegiance to, 98, 101
    attendance, frequency of, 67, 71, 81,
    83
    automobile driving, 91, 111
    impacts of racial change, 3-4, 98
    membership status, 128-129
    metropolitan housing policies, and,
    138-139, 142
    political action, 128
    social action, 121
    stabilization efforts, 24, 120-133,
    140-142

Wynnefield, 39

Taeuber, Karl and Alma, 1, 14-15, 26
Telephone interviews, 8, 143, 147-148
Tenant-landlord relationship, 28-29
Tenant status, *see* Homeownership
Thompson, Wilbur, 5, 136
Tipping point, 21, 27, 34-35
Tobin, Gary, 6, 17n., 18n., 27
Turks, 14

United States Department of Housing and
    Urban Development, 84, 137
United States National Advisory
    Commission on Civil Disorders, 2
United States Supreme Court, 136n.,
    137n.
Urban renewal, 3

Vacant homes, 58-60, 65
Van Arsdol, Maurice D. Jr., 85
Vandalism, 28-29, 61
Violence, 34, 141-142

Washington, D.C., 2, 29
    Adams-Morgan, 1
    Georgetown, 1
    Prince Georges County (Maryland), 2
    Shepherd Park, 18
Washington Township, New Jersey, 137n.
Welfare, 26, 53
Whites
    black-white differences, 16, 25-26,
    27, 30-31, 36, 38, 48-56, 65
    black-white social contacts, 1-2, 65,
    66, 88n., 112
    integrated communities, desired
    features of, 100, 134-135
    inter-ethnic group tensions, 4; *see
    also* Ethnicity
    panic moves, 1n., 5, 15, 16, 17n., 21,
    23, 27-28, 29, 39, 67-68, 73, 81, 83,
    103-104, 134, 139
    reactions to black inmigration, 15,
    20-21, 34, 64, 141-142
    stereotypes of blacks, 23-24, 36, 88n.
Wilkes, Paul, 31
Willingboro, New Jersey, 5
Wilmington, Delaware, 138
Wirth, Louis, 14

Wolf, Eleanor P., 18-19, 21, 22-23, 27,
    70, 98n.
Working class communities, 17, 36
Wynnefield
    boundaries, 8, 10, 40n.
    Catholics, 39, 46
    crime, 61-63, 65, 104, 107-108, 111,
    118, 135
    history, 38-48
    housing conditions, 40, 46, 48, 58-60,
    63, 69-70, 78, 97-98, 101, 107,
    112-113, 139
    housing search, 105, 109-119, 135
    housing type and density, 8, 11, 12
    location, 8
    Lower Hill section, 39, 40, 47, 59,
    69, 95, 100-101, 134-135
    neighborhoods, 8, 69-70
    population size, 8
    property values, 61, 78, 80, 113
    rates of transition, 40, 45, 46, 48, 56,
    58, 70, 136

real estate brokers, 45, 46, 136
reasons for moving, 103-109,
    118-119, 134-135, 140
schools, 43, 56-59, 65, 69, 79, 104,
    107, 109-110, 123-124, 133
socio-economic characteristics, 48-56
synagogues, 39
Upper Hill section, 46, 48, 56, 58,
    59, 69-70, 78, 79n., 97-98, 101,
    112-113, 116, 139
white panic moves, 67-68, 73, 81, 83,
    134,
    see also Apartments, Blacks,
    Detached homes, Racial Transition
    Process
Wynnefield Development Council of
    Organizations, 43
Wynnefield Residents Association, 45-46,
    64, 136

Zehner, Robert B., 2, 17
Zoning, 16, 45, 137n., 142n.